Daughter, Your Faith Has Healed You!

by
Bonita Chase Darby

Bloomington, IN  Milton Keynes, UK

authorHOUSE®

AuthorHouse™
1663 Liberty Drive, Suite 200
Bloomington, IN 47403
www.authorhouse.com
Phone: 1-800-839-8640

AuthorHouse™ UK Ltd.
500 Avebury Boulevard
Central Milton Keynes, MK9 2BE
www.authorhouse.co.uk
Phone: 08001974150

First published by AuthorHouse 10/6/2006

ISBN: 1-4259-5592-4 (sc)

Printed in the United States of America
Bloomington, Indiana

This book is printed on acid-free paper.

Scripture quotations are taken from The Holy Bible, New King James Version, King James Version, New International Version

For information regarding seminars, workshops and copies of
Daughter, Your Faith Has Healed You! Contact:
Fighting Abuse In The Home (F.A.I.T.H.)
Campbell Chapel AME Church
1500 E. 22nd Avenue
Denver, CO 80205
(303) 839-5058
Or fiaministries@msn.com

SPECIAL APPRECIATION AND ACKNOWLEDGEMENTS

To my daughter – *Gina, thank you. You were and continue to be, my reason for living. You saved my life. If it weren't for you, I would have given up. My heart bursts with love for you and I could never put into words how proud I am of you. God truly blessed me when He allowed me to be your mother.*

To my husband – *John, thank you for drying my tears when the memories came rushing back, and your love and understanding when I wanted to be alone.*

To my mother — *Mom, thank you for allowing me to lean on you. You kept telling me that this experience was all part of a plan that God had for me and that I should not give up. I know it wasn't easy for you knowing what was happening, but you kept the faith and you continued to pray. You were right! I am blessed to be your daughter.*

To Rev. Dr. Jacqueline G. Reeves – *Thank you for your love and spiritual teaching. I never thought I would meet such a person as you. I thank God for putting you in my life. Thank you for being my spiritual mother.*

To Faith In Action Intercessory Prayer Ministries, Inc. – I could never express how much you mean to me. Thank you for all your prayers, love, and gentle "pushing."

To my sisters who are in abusive relationships – Don't give up. God is not finished. Turn your situation completely over to Him. Always remember that Jesus came to set the captives free, and you shall be free. Be assured that you are not alone and there is hope. **I am a living witness!**

To my anointed angel of an editor – Nanette Snipes. Thank you for bringing my story to life. I am convinced that God sent you at the "appointed time."

DEDICATION

This book is dedicated to all who have experienced abusive relationships. It also speaks to those who know someone in an abusive relationship. While this is a book about domestic abuse, it was prompted by the Holy Spirit. I pray through this book you will be healed and delivered as it ministers to you. May God fill you with blessings.

"And suddenly, a woman who had a flow of blood for twelve years came from behind and touched the hem of His garment. For she said to herself, 'If only I may touch His garment, I shall be made well.' But Jesus turned around, and when He saw her He said, 'Be of good cheer, daughter; your faith has made you well.' And the woman was made well from that hour" (Matt. 9:20-22, NKJV).

This woman had searched for help but to no avail. She had seen many physicians. They took her money but couldn't heal her. She couldn't understand why she had to suffer. What had she done to deserve this? She had no friends, and her family had deserted her. People mocked her and shouted, "Unclean!" whenever she appeared. She felt alone and was about to give up.

But grace and mercy prevailed. She learned that Jesus was in town. She had heard so much about Him. He healed the blind who regained their sight and the lame who jumped and leapt, praising Him. If He did it for others, He could surely heal her. She never dreamed she could get close to Him, but she felt in her heart that if she could touch Him she would be healed.

The woman knew Jesus represented healing, love, deliverance—everything she needed. Although she felt unloved at times, she felt that Jesus loved her in spite of everything. And through His love, she would be healed. She pushed her way through the crowd, fell on her face before the Lord and touched the hem of Jesus' garment. Immediately, she was healed. Another woman had an issue. It wasn't a serious issue of blood; it was an issue of domestic violence.

She was physically and mentally abused, but she couldn't seek help from doctors or friends. If her husband found out she asked for help, he might kill her. She never talked to anyone, because she thought no one would believe her. She resigned herself to the knowledge that she was alone. There was nowhere to turn and no one to turn to. What could she do?

Occasionally when she had tried to tell someone, the person changed the subject. Oftentimes, she felt as though she were losing her mind. She had to find help somewhere, but where? She finally cried out to Jesus, whom she had heard about when she was a child, and He heard her cries. She, oh so gently, touched the hem of His garment in prayer, and He healed her. But, it didn't end there. Now, she needs to tell everyone of a loving God who brought her out of the wilderness of domestic violence into the Promised Land of ministry. By touching the hem of the Lord's garment, she was healed just as others can be.

I rushed Gina into the bathroom and gave her a quick bath and hurried her into her room to put on her school uniform. Noticing her rumpled hair, I said, "Gina, come in my room. I want to fix your hair."

The noise behind me made me turn quickly. When I looked, Frank's eyes narrowed and he scowled at me.

"Frank, what's wrong? Why are you looking at me like that?" He had one hand behind his back and when he pulled it out, he held the gun I thought he'd gotten rid of years before. Without a word, he held the gun to my head. He looked over his shoulder as though he were awaiting instructions from an unseen being.

"It's over, baby," he said. "This is for you and what you've done to me."

I looked into his eyes, and I knew this was the turning point.

Please, God, don't let Gina see me die like this. Let me get her out of the house. Please . . .

Gina was almost eight years old, and I didn't want her to spend the rest of her life remembering my dying in front of her.

Just the night before, I had poured out my heart to God and asked for His help. I believed with all my heart that I would not be harmed. I had felt His presence.

Oh, Lord, I know you are with me. You won't let me die. Father, protect me. What about my baby? What will happen to her?

My mother's love poured out, and as usual, Gina sensed my distress. She crawled into my lap, and she gazed into my eyes. I hugged her, and then tried to put her down, but she wouldn't turn loose of me. It was as if she knew that if she stayed, nothing would happen. Her father would never hurt me as long as I was holding her.

I turned Gina around so that she faced me and had her back to her father.

I want her face to be the last thing I see, and if she has to be here, I hope the Lord wipes this memory from her.

Frank looked over his shoulder again as if he were listening to someone behind him. Then he shook his head. Slowly, it came to me that I was in a fight for my soul. It was the age-old fight between God and Satan, and I knew who would win. God had already told me He would fight my battles. I had to believe and trust Him. I had experienced so much, but I knew God would never leave me. He promised He wouldn't.

Frank put the gun to my head, and I knew he was going to pull the trigger. As his finger tightened on the trigger, I started to remember the past few years. *How did I get to this point? What happened?*

Table of Contents

Chapter 1

I awoke early that Saturday filled with excitement. The sun shone through my window, and I could feel its warmth. I heard the birds chirping in the courtyard that connected the two apartment buildings. All at once it hit me! No wonder I was so happy. It was my wedding day! I jumped out of bed and grabbed a hairbrush. I brushed through my hair, then began singing into it and dancing in my bedroom. It was hard to believe. I was nineteen years old, something my mother said to me several times as I planned my wedding. In a few hours, I would be a married woman, setting up my own apartment. I had worked things out in my mind, and things were going just the way they should.

I had landed a government job right out of high school and planned to attend college to pursue my dream of becoming a nurse. I was so happy that I felt guilty. Was it possible for one person to have so much at such a young age? My life was perfect. I fell back on the bed and laughed thinking how my mother's friend had said, "You're too young to get married. You have your whole life ahead of you." Someone even asked if I was pregnant.

They only needed to know my mother to know I wasn't pregnant. She had put the fear of God into me about "bringing home babies," and how my body was not something to be used and discarded. She taught me all about respecting myself and setting down rules at the beginning of my marriage so there would be no mistakes.

I thought of my future husband, Frank. We were so happy being with each other that people would stop and stare because there was such radiance around us. He had a movie star smile, and anyone could tell that he took his time making sure his clothes and hair looked impeccable. The finished product was almost perfect.

When I first met Frank, some of his female friends laughed. "You are just a baby." "Aren't you still in school?" "Frank is too much of a man for you." "You wouldn't even know what to do with him!" They were jealous because he had chosen a much younger woman. Well, I laughed last.

Today, we would be married, and I couldn't wait to see their faces as I walked down the aisle. I made sure to invite all his friends who thought I was "too young to hold a man like Frank." What would they say now? I knew they would be full of envy, but it would be too late for them to do anything about it. The women who had laughed about my being so young wouldn't laugh today.

I was young, but Frank and I would be husband and wife, and according to the Bible, "For this cause shall a man leave father and mother, and shall cleave to his wife; and they twain shall be one flesh? Wherefore they are no more twain, but one flesh. What therefore God hath joined together, let not man put asunder" (Matt. 19:5.6, KJV). I was confident that because we made the commitment to be man and wife before God Almighty that He would keep us together as one, and no one could ever separate us.

I looked around my bare room. Only my bed, dresser, and phone remained. I had moved my things the night before, and nothing showed I had even lived in the apartment with my mother, brother, and sister.

I still couldn't believe that, after my wedding, I would not be returning. Instead I would go to my new home with my new husband. My sister couldn't wait. She would get my room.

My husband . . . it had a nice ring to it. By tonight I would be a wife! This would be the beginning of a new life for me. I was both happy and frightened at the same time. I was thrilled to become Frank's wife, but what if I wasn't a good one?

"Frank," I'd said, "Do you think I'll make a good wife?" I watched his smile turn into a laugh.

"I've never been a husband before, and I guess we'll just have to learn together."

I looked forward to the learning experience. I knew we would have fun learning from each other, laughing at each other's mistakes.

"Are you awake, honey?" Mommy stood at the door with two full laundry baskets. "I don't care what day it is, you still have to get the laundry done," she said.

When Mommy said "Jump," I always thought, "How high?" So here I was on my wedding day, walking to the Laundromat, pulling a cart full of clothes.

I saw some people who would be attending the wedding. I could see the laughter shining in their eyes. I know they thought it was humorous that I was washing clothes, but it still remained my responsibility—for one last day.

Besides, it took my mind off the wedding for a while. The butterflies in my stomach were beginning to flutter, and I was trying hard not to notice.

When I left the Laundromat, I heard the owner shout, "See ya next week!"

"No, you won't. I'm getting married," I said.

"How old are you? Sixteen?" she asked. "Are you sure you're old enough to get married?"

I put one hand on my hip and flipped my hair with the other. "I am nineteen years old!"

"I wish you well, girl," she said. The way she said it made me wonder if she really meant it. What was wrong with people? They acted as if it was a crime to get married at nineteen. I was old enough to know what I wanted, and I wanted to be married to Frank.

As I pulled the heavy cart home I thought, "One of the first things I plan to do is buy a washing machine and dryer."

The day was perfect. The sky was a powder blue and small clouds seemed to slide effortlessly across the wide expanse. I drew in a deep breath. The day couldn't be better for my wedding.

I remember smiling. *God is happy with me. He sent a wonderful wedding day. What do those people know? Why can't people stop talking about my age and just be happy for me?*

After folding the clothes, I would soon get ready at my friend's apartment and be transformed into a bride. I put away the last piece of laundry. Then I turned, looked around the apartment and said good-bye.

I felt a knot grow in my stomach. It wasn't butterflies; it wasn't nervousness; it was fear. It was as if someone were saying, "Stop! Don't do this!"

For a moment, I wanted to run to my mother and say she was right all along. I didn't want to get married. But the feeling passed, and I felt it was probably pre-marital jitters.

In hindsight, I wished I'd listen to the voice—the Holy Spirit. But I had never experienced a check in my spirit from Him, so I ignored Him.

When I walked out of the apartment, a drop of rain splashed the ground loudly, then another and another. It seemed as if the clouds opened up. Without warning, the ground filled with large puddles. In moments, thunder boomed and lightning lit up the darkened skies. *Maybe I shouldn't get married. No, that's just silly . . . and superstitious.*

When I arrived at my friend's apartment, I was soaking wet. I couldn't believe it. *What happened to my beautiful day?* I guessed God was cleaning the street so the world would look fresh and clean for my special day. I never thought for a moment how I was justifying my actions in front of God.

Outside, I heard cars driving through standing water. I took a quick shower and dried my hair.

I will not let this awful downpour bother me. I put on my wedding gown, lightly brushed my hair and touched up my lipstick. Almost as soon as the photographer arrived, he began to take pictures. Not long afterwards the wedding party arrived and the weather was no longer a concern to me. In fact, I was convinced that the sun would soon come out.

I can't believe it. I'm actually getting married. I pinched myself. It wasn't a dream. My bridesmaids walked down the stairs singing loudly and out of tune, then they burst into laughter. My father met me with an umbrella at the apartment, and for a few minutes, I felt an unusual chill, but not because of the rain or cold. It was that same strange feeling

I'd had earlier. Maybe I was just nervous. What else could it be? I was headstrong and planned to get married despite my odd feelings.

On the way to the church, the visibility was almost zero, and the chauffeur had to drive slowly. When we arrived at the church, water flooded the steps, and people waited at their cars until someone came with an umbrella to shield them.

When I turned to get out of the car, I felt that ominous chill again. *What is wrong with me?* Was I getting sick on my wedding day? Was it a warning? I knew that whatever it was, it wasn't normal, but then I had never gotten married before, either. It has to be my nerves.

The Lord continued trying to talk to me, but I wasn't listening. He was knocking on the door, but I wasn't answering. Many of us don't want to listen when we are getting a word from the Lord, but if we would just be still, He will speak.

"This is it," I thought. There's no turning back. Everyone is at the church and waiting for me. When I arrived at the church, I saw my uncle, who was like a father to me, crying. His body shuddered because he was crying so loud. Tears lined his face and, for a few moments, I hesitated. When I walked down the aisle, I noticed people's expressions. Some people rolled their eyes, and I knew they were thinking, "I can't believe she is getting married. She's way too young."

But my friends were smiling and giving the peace sign. In spite of the mixed messages I received, this was my day, and I felt like a queen.

While I stood in the receiving line, I hugged my uncle. "Don't worry. I'm a married woman now. Everything is going to be all right." He cried even harder. He held me tight, like he didn't want to ever let go. He was a strong man of God, and I feel that, through him, God was crying tears of joy for me.

When I left the church, a woman met me at the bottom of the church steps and said, "For every drop of rain that falls today, that's how many tears you will cry during this marriage."

Jealous old woman; I don't have time for you. "Death and life are in the power of the tongue" (Prov. 18:21a, KJV). Her message could have been a warning. Whatever it was, it was too late to change anything.

The ceremony was beautiful and when I said my vows, I promised God and myself that I would love Frank and be his wife forever, until death parted us, and I meant it. I believed nothing could break up our marriage. After all, I had stood before God and promised Him that I would keep my vows.

By the time Frank and I arrived at the reception hall, I had forgotten about my strange feelings and the words of the old woman about how my marriage would fail.

I was married. I had a husband and all was right with the world. I was glad to see many friends who had graduated with me the previous year, and we reminisced about the good times, especially during our senior year. We promised each other that we would always stay in touch. "Girl, we will always be best friends and nothing will ever come between us." "We're going to talk at least once a week."

I took a quick look around the reception hall at the two groups. It was strange. The hall seemed to be separated; the young people (my friends) on one side, and the older ones (Frank's friends) on the other. It was like two different worlds trying hard to come together, but not quite making it. Later on, I remembered the gap between us and when it started.

Finally, the reception ended and people began to leave. A crowd formed in the vestibule, and many of the guests turned around and came back inside. While we had been dancing, a winter storm blew in. I ran to the front of the reception hall and opened the door. A cold, wet gust of wind blasted my face. The rain had stopped, but in its place was several inches of snow.

That snowstorm turned out to be one of the worst blizzards ever to hit New York, and we were snowbound. The taxis and limos left hours before, stranding many of the guests. Those who had cars took as many passengers as they could to their homes. Some made return trips to take people home because of the transportation shutdown.

After what seemed like hours, Frank and I were finally able to leave. One of my uncles drove us home. I had never seen or heard of anything like it—New York City had literally shut down! For the next few days, there was no transportation. I really didn't mind because I spent time with my new husband. I knew we wouldn't have any surprise company, because there was no way for anyone to get around with all the snow, which seemed to stick around longer than usual.

During the week, we opened our wedding gifts. I was excited about each gift but disappointed that Frank seemed impatient with my enthusiasm. *Maybe he's just tired.* I would open a gift and shout, "Oh, just what we needed!" Every gift gave me great joy, but Frank seemed to be annoyed. When I asked him if he was all right, he'd smile and say he was just thinking about our new lives.

We decided against a honeymoon because I had not been working long enough for a vacation. But we planned to go away at a later date.

It didn't bother me because I knew someday soon we would be able to afford a trip to the Caribbean. With both of us working, we should be able to have the honeymoon of our dreams. When I told Frank, he smiled oddly and said, "That's what I've been thinking. We'll travel the whole world." He assured me he would work hard so that when we took our vacations, we would be able to afford the best hotels, entertainment, and food. *Nothing but the best for us, baby!*

With snow several feet deep outside, I cooked some of Frank's favorite foods. I wanted to take care of my new home and wanted everything to be perfect. The apartment filled with the aroma of home-cooked meals with dinner rolls or cornbread baking in the oven. Because of Frank's preferences, I cooked only fresh vegetables instead of canned.

"Hey Frank," I said one day. "I think I'll go to the vegetable stand for some fresh vegetables."

"Look, I don't want any of that stuff. Don't you bring any of that leafy, green lettuce or vegetables home."

"But, Frank . . ." I stopped short. I didn't want to start anything. I was just the opposite of him. I only liked green, leafy lettuce and vegetables. *Well, if he doesn't want them, I'll just cook some for myself.*

"Did you hear me? I don't want none of that stuff brought into this house. I don't like them, or the way they smell!"

As time ticked on, Frank was adamant about certain things. He wouldn't eat certain vegetables and wanted some of his meals cooked in a specific way. For example, he loved beef liver, and it had to be cooked just right with onions or he would get upset. *Not a problem. He has a right to say what he likes.* What was beginning to bother me was, although he didn't like the same foods I did, he said they were not "allowed" in the house. *Not allowed? Hey, I live here too.*

Not only didn't Frank allow certain foods in the house, he demanded how he wanted his clothes washed and ironed. He refused to use tissues, but had to have starched and ironed handkerchiefs for his pocket at all times. As I began to know Frank better, I realized that he could be very demanding and moody, but in my eyes, there was no danger in that. After all, everyone has a bad day now and then. So I ignored his mood swings and made up my mind that I would keep him happy.

Chapter II

The sun seemed to shine brighter than usual that morning. I didn't get right out of the bed and wanted to lie there marveling at what a beautiful day it would be.

I've been married a year now. I'll bet all those people who said it wouldn't work are surprised. We made it! Life is beautiful and our marriage is wonderful.

In spite of Frank's increasing mood swings, this year was one of the happiest ones of my life. Frank was attentive—the greatest husband any woman could have.

Many times he surprised me with flowers, jewelry, or clothing. I never knew what he held behind his back when he came home with that mysterious smile. During those times, I felt excited when I heard his key click in the door. I greeted him with open arms. He always expected his hug and kiss as soon as the door opened. Later, it no longer would be what he expected, but what he demanded.

As we sat at the table, preparing to eat our "anniversary breakfast," I was overwhelmed with my feelings of love for my husband. I loved him more than ever.

"I didn't think anyone could be this happy, Frank." I smiled at him from across the table. "No one could be this happy, could they?"

An enigmatic smile crossed his lips. I wondered what he really thought.

Sometimes, his friends called us "lovebirds" because we were always together, holding hands, and always smiling. Whenever we went to a party or a dance, we would be inseparable, only dancing or sitting with each other.

He makes me feel so special, especially when he protects me. I love how he walks me to the ladies' room, so I won't get lost. I bet not many men do that for their wives.

I knew some of his friends were womanizers and didn't know if they liked the "new" Frank. "Hey man, what happened? You got married and now you're someone else. You're not as much fun as you used to be."

"You're just jealous," he'd say to them, "'cause I found someone. I've changed. Those things I did in the past are history," he said.

"What things, Frank?" He'd shoot me a look that felt like a dagger, and I'd shudder. Just as quickly, his countenance changed back to the smiling, handsome man I married.

The Bible warns that Satan is deceptive, a liar, and a murderer. He wants to destroy God's people. He also has an uncontrollable rage because his time is short, and he is determined to destroy. "The thief comes only to steal and kill and destroy; I have come that they may have life, and have it to the full" (John 10:10, NIV).

I never thought Frank was capable of showing a rage that would make me run for my life. I only saw the handsome, caring man that was always by my side—my angel. Don't let anyone fool you. Satan is real! He wants all of God's people to die, and he won't stop trying as long as we are alive. I know now that it was all part of a plan to destroy me and prevent my ministry.

The year had gone by quickly. It seemed as if we had only been married a few months. When our anniversary drew near, we made plans to go out for dinner and a movie. I bought a special dress to wear for the occasion. I couldn't wait. We made it to a year in spite of the negative words and thoughts directed at us from those who said our marriage was a mistake. Everything was going just fine.

I felt some anxiety as I stood at the kitchen table wrapping Frank's anniversary gift. *Why do I feel anxious? Is it because he's been picky lately? Maybe I'm not a good wife. I'll try harder.*

Sometimes Frank got a look on his face that I couldn't understand. Was he happy, sad, angry, or just thinking? People told me that someday

I would be able to look at him and tell exactly what he was thinking. Maybe if I had known what he was thinking, I could have changed my situation before it turned dangerous.

When the doorbell rang that late December day, I answered it.

"Nana, what a wonderful surprise!" I couldn't believe she'd stopped by with an anniversary surprise for me—my cousin who had just returned from Vietnam.

I was glad to see him looking healthy and happy. During the time he'd spent overseas, I had been afraid something would happen to him, yet here he was on my first wedding anniversary. What a wonderful present!

Frank had been in a bad mood all day, and I felt this visit would make him happy. He liked family, or so I thought at the time.

I was surprised to see my grandmother because she rarely ever visited or called me. She and my mother were estranged and there were few good memories of her.

By coming to my house, maybe it meant she was making the first step toward reconciliation. After all, we were granddaughter and grandmother and we should have a relationship. Wrong! The visit went well for a while, and then my grandmother began to make insulting comments about my mother.

She came into *my* home and insulted *my* mother. For a few moments, I just sat there on the sofa in amazement. Frank said nothing.

What is wrong with you? You are insulting someone I love dearly—my mother. You have a lot of nerve talking about my mother like that.

Surely this couldn't be happening. I had been raised to respect my elders and hesitated saying what was really on my mind. I could feel my temper rising, and it was getting harder to control my tongue. For a while, I shut down and refused to say anything, but she kept on talking. The more she talked, the angrier I got.

Finally, I couldn't hold out any longer, and I heard myself shout, "How dare you talk about my mother! You have to leave. NOW!" I rarely ever raised my voice, and I was shocked I even did it. In fact my classmates in school laughed at me because the teachers could hardly hear me. Throughout the years, I developed a reputation of telling someone off, and people never even knew because they couldn't quite hear me. But I had never shown that side of me to my family.

My visitors made a hasty retreat. I was glad they left, because I didn't want my day ruined any further. This was our anniversary, and no one was supposed to interrupt, much less interfere. I wanted to spend time alone with my husband on this special day.

It saddened me to see my cousin leave. I had so many things I wanted to ask him. He had been in a war, seen people he knew die or shot and he was so young; in his early twenties. He left with my grandmother giving me a "I know what you mean, but I can't do anything about it" look.

After I heard the front door close, I started the water for my bath, put my clothes on the bed, and prepared myself for our evening. Frank had walked out with my grandmother and cousin, but when he returned, he had that same enigmatic look I'd begun to see often.

I smoothed out the clothes and turned to say something. The slap came swiftly and stung the side of my face.

I slapped him back. "Don't you ever put your hands on me again!"

He responded by hitting me hard in the ear with his fist. "If you ever speak to anyone in your family like that again, I will do more than this."

I refused to back down. I lunged at him, and he pushed me back. I was nobody's punching bag. I would not only fight back, but I would make sure my family knew that he hit me. It was as though he read my mind.

"You better keep your mouth shut about this," he said. "Don't even think of telling your family."

His eyes looked bloodshot, and he screamed at me. "You better not say anything, or I'll kill you and your family! I know where they live. They'll never know I did it, because you'll already be dead. His eyes narrowed and his jaw was set in controlled anger. "If you don't believe me, try it again."

Every part of me said to run as fast as I could, but I hesitated. I wanted to reason with him and ask him why he was so angry. I was also angry and wanted to get back at him.

Surely he didn't mean what he said. What kind of crazy person is he? Oh, he'll pay for this. I won't talk to him.

This was so unlike the Frank I knew. This was some insane person. Why did he take my grandmother's side? He didn't even know her, but he knew my mother. He was sitting right next to me during the conversation. *What was going on?*

When I finally got over being angry, confusion and fear took its place as Frank's words began to sink in. *Was he going crazy? Did I miss something? He had threatened to kill me! What was I supposed to do now? I knew he meant what he said, and I didn't want my family hurt. I felt panic gnaw in my stomach.*

Frank's demeanor changed. As quickly as he turned angry, he became pensive. "Let's go out and celebrate our anniversary," he said. *What? Is he kidding?*

"I'm so glad we're married. Baby, I'm sorry I got so upset. Let's just put this behind us." He smiled really big, and for a moment, I believed he meant it.

In the cycle of domestic violence, Frank was beginning what's known as The Honeymoon Stage—when the abuser is remorseful and convinces the victim he is sorry and shows signs of love, such as bringing flowers, candy, etc.

He became excited about the evening and talked about the movie and our dinner.

My mind raced. *How can he change like that? He was full of rage one minute, and the next, a loving husband.*

Surely he didn't think I was going to dinner and a movie after what happened. I put my clothes back in the closet, put on some jeans and went into the kitchen to prepare a meal, determined that the discussion wasn't over. I waited for both of us to calm down.

I'll just tell him I'm leaving unless he gets some help. I refuse to allow anyone to hit me like that.

"What are you doing?" Frank bellowed. "I said, 'We're going to dinner and a movie.' You better be ready in fifteen minutes!"

My heart pounded so loud in my chest I was afraid Frank could hear it. I quickly looked around. Somehow I had backed into a position I could not get out of without passing him. I was trapped. Frank seemed changed—even his features became hardened, his eyes narrowed and his mouth twisted in anger.

I backed up as much as I could. *Oh, my God! I'm trapped. There's no place for me to go.* Everything I'd planned to say stuck in my throat. Frank shoved me—hard. He wanted to show that he was serious.

"I'm not going anywhere with you. You have a problem! You need help. Are you crazy?"

His rage became uncontrollable. Repeatedly, he hit me with closed fists. The blows landed on my face, my chest, my arms, my back; almost any place he could pound. I hoped I would lose consciousness, so I wouldn't feel the beating, but it didn't happen. I felt every blow until I was almost numb. I was so weak I couldn't fight back; my body wouldn't let me.

I gritted my teeth. *As God is my witness, this will never happen again. This will be the first and last time.* I had to get out, but I thought he was going to kill me before I had a chance. I had been raised in a household where there was no violence. I hadn't even been spanked. *Please, God. Make him stop. The pain is unbearable! Make him stop!*

What seemed like hours later, I stepped into the bathtub, barely lifting my leg over the side. The effort brought waves of pain. I felt as if I would black out. I had to fight to keep my eyes open. I eased into the hot water, feeling some relief, but I was hurting so much, I became dizzy.

The pounding on the bathroom door startled me.

"Don't take all night! We have to go!" His voice frightened me and I cringed, but hurried because I didn't want him to attack me again. If he started beating me again, I felt I wouldn't survive. I couldn't bear any more. I knew that. He moved through a variety of emotions: anger, peace, joy . . . It was unbelievable. If the bathroom had had a back door, I would have used it.

I walked out of my bathroom clinging to the wall to ease the pain and to keep my balance while Frank stood there, fully dressed, with a smile on his face. He noticed I was bending over because of the pain, and the smile disappeared.

He wasn't sorry; he was impatient. He felt I was moving too slowly. When he glared at me like that, I knew I had to move quicker or he would go into another rage. Despite the pain, I began to get dressed, but had to stop from time to time to place my hand on the wall so I wouldn't faint.

Please don't let me faint. He'll kill me if I do. If I hurry and don't aggravate him, maybe he'll leave me alone.

Part of me was still trying to figure out what had happened. I didn't know this man. *What could have set him off like this?* Maybe something awful had happened, and he couldn't handle it. I knew that was no excuse, but I wanted to understand. Maybe if I had been nicer and kept my mouth shut; maybe if I hadn't been so defiant; maybe. . .

I moved around the room, and I caught a glimpse of myself in the mirror. I couldn't believe the ugly, red marks beginning to surface on my body. My face was not marked considering the beating it took, and I remember thinking, "Well, at least I don't have to explain anything."

Fortunately it was December, and I could wear long sleeves, but those sleeves could never hide the pain in my heart. I was hurt and in shock.

"Why did I have to open my mouth? Why couldn't I have been quiet?" *Had I pushed him to his limit? What had I done?*

In the midst of pain and suffering, women in abusive relationships blame themselves for the violence although it is not their fault. Yet, in the midst of their pain and denial, they will try to explain away the violence.

I retraced my remarks and still felt I was right. I had heard of women who had been beaten by boyfriends, but never their husbands.

This will never happen again. I will make sure. I'll do everything right, I'll be a better wife and a better person. How could someone who had taken a vow before God to honor and love me, do such a thing? I didn't know it, but even in the midst of the fight when I thought I might die, God was with me.

We finally went out. As the night progressed, the previous event seemed to be something that had happened to someone else. Frank seemed to be enjoying himself, and I was determined not to say any more about what had happened until the next day. I planned to pack my clothes, and when he came home from work, be gone. I wasn't sure how I would explain the incident, and I wasn't even sure if I should go to my mother's home. I still had some friends I could talk to, but I would have to be honest with them. They also knew my family. *What if they said something and Frank found out? Was I trapped?*

While riding the train home, fear began to rise in my throat. When the train passed Franklin Avenue where my mother lived, I wanted to jump off the train and run to my mother.

If I move fast enough, maybe I can outrun Frank. Maybe if I just begin to scream, someone will help me. But, Frank's threat to kill my family echoed in my ears and when the train doors closed, it was as if they smiled at me saying, "You can't go anywhere." *Will this nightmare ever end? Will I ever wake up?*

When we returned home and were getting ready for bed, he turned to me and said, "I don't want to hurt you. You just made me hit you."

Once again, I opened my mouth. "But I didn't do anything, Frank." I held my breath a moment, and then added, "I'm not letting anyone talk about my mother that way. And you had no right to hit me no matter what I did."

He balled up his fist and hit me again. He must have realized how badly he'd hurt me earlier, because he stopped. I was determined that, when he went to sleep, I would walk out of his life. His threats didn't frighten me. It was just talk.

Again, he seemed to read my mind. He stepped into the closet and pulled out a gun. "Do you see this gun? If you even think about leaving, I will find you and kill you. Remember, no one will believe you, or even think I did it. If you don't believe me, just try!" The look in his eyes was pure hatred. He meant every word, and I knew it. I thought he was going to kill me right then and there, but he put the gun in his pocket, turned and walked away.

When did he get a gun? I didn't even know he had one. At that moment, I wanted to pick up something, hit him in the head and leave his body lying there, or better still, take his own gun and kill him.

How could I think of such a horrible plan? I couldn't kill anyone, or could I?

You must never give Satan ground. Just like the thoughts that entered my mind, he will plant thoughts in your mind and before you know it, you have given in. We are to take every thought captive as it says in 2 Cor.10:5, NIV: "We demolish arguments and every pretension that sets itself up against the knowledge of God, and we take captive every thought to make it obedient to Christ."

Later, I put on my nightgown, crawled into bed and closed my eyes afraid that this was going to be my last night on earth. I wanted to forget this awful day. But it was our first anniversary—a day to remember—both good and bad. This was the beginning of my journey through hell.

The next morning, I roused from a deep sleep. On becoming somewhat awake, pain shot through me like an arrow. My legs throbbed as though they'd been broken. I groaned every time I moved. My whole head and face felt the size of a basketball. I gingerly touched my cheeks.

I had still not fully awakened and struggled to open my eyes. *What is wrong with me? Why do I feel as though I have the flu? Why does my body seem to be rebelling?*

My mind began to clear, and like a shot, the memory of the previous night rocketed in.

I remembered his balled-up fists streaking across my line of vision. Again and again, Frank had pounded my head, my face, my entire body. I had crossed my arms in front of me and shivered, afraid to open my eyes.

My heart began pounding with the memory. *Is he still beside me? I dare not move if he is.* I turned my head slightly and opened one eye. The bed was empty. I felt relieved. *I hope he never comes back.*

The pain increased as I pulled the covers off and stepped onto the floor. I noticed blood on the sheet. *Do I have internal injuries? Could he have beaten me that badly?*

In the bathroom mirror, I stared at the strange face looking back at me. My whole face was swollen. There were bruised places on my arms and legs, and everything hurt.

The sound of footsteps on the stairs made me shudder. *Oh, God, please help me. He's coming back.*

I began to visibly tremble when he opened the door.

"Hey, I just went down to the restaurant and got you some breakfast." He smiled at me as though nothing had ever happened.

"You deserve to be treated like a queen. No cooking for you today," he said.

Very slowly, I made my way to the kitchen.

Tears clouded his eyes. "I'm so sorry, baby. I promise I'll never hurt you again. I promise." He touched my arm lovingly, but I winced, not knowing what he was going to do. "Please forgive me."

I sat down and pulled the food and drink from the bag. I didn't look up. I couldn't; I was afraid.

"If you want, I'll even take you to the hospital. Just say the words, baby, I'll do whatever you want."

I wanted so badly to believe everything he said. I had never seen a man cry before and believed he must have been truly sorry.

How did it ever come to this? He had been the perfect gentleman while we were dating. What happened to the man I knew?

He said he'd gotten rid of the gun, and he would never hurt me again.

With a smile on his face, the old Frank I used to know called my job to tell them I wouldn't be in for a few days.

He wouldn't let me do a thing. He prepared my meals, and then brought them to me. He helped me get into and out of the shower. Quite simply, I was pampered.

He must really love me. Look at all he's doing for me. All I have to do is get better.

In fact, he was so attentive the thought never crossed my mind that there was a deceitful bone in his body. The memory of the horror began to diminish.

Late one afternoon while the sun was still overhead, and our house was filled with its warmth, I looked into Frank's eyes and all I could see was love. I was tempted to kiss him, but I held back.

How can he be the embodiment of love today when just a couple of days ago, he had beaten me like an animal? How can he change so suddenly?

When I looked into his eyes that day, the love that shone in his eyes practically erased all the hate and rage I now knew lived within him.

Days passed, and we got on with our lives. At night, though, I sometimes awoke in a sweat not sure if I had been dreaming or not. It all seemed so unreal. Perspiration would drench my nightgown, and it stuck to my body.

When Frank turned over in bed, I wondered if he would attack me again, and I would shrink away. Sometimes my eyes suddenly popped open, and I checked his side of the bed to be sure he was asleep.

One night, I awoke with a start. *The gun! Where is the gun? He said he'd gotten rid of it, but I don't believe him.*

When I got up the next morning I searched the house for the weapon but never found it. Uneasiness rode my shoulders, and I felt helpless. Frank could easily turn into that monster again and with one quick pull of the trigger, I'd be gone. I needed to talk to someone about my fears, but who would listen? More importantly, who would believe me?

After a couple of weeks, the pain and bruises began to heal, along with the memory of the beating. I justified everything he did.

It wasn't that bad. Frank promised he would never again hurt me. Besides, I must've somehow provoked him to such rage. I'll just be a good wife, keep my mouth shut, and he won't have any reason to hit me. I'll change so much that he'll love me again, and he'll never again look at me with hate in his eyes.

But, although I was going to try harder I asked myself, *What have I gotten myself into?*

Chapter III

While living in this apartment, I had two wonderful neighbors. I met Marcy before Frank and I married. She lived on the same floor as I, and when Frank introduced me as his bride-to-be, she was genuinely happy for me.

Marcy was gentle and had a warm smile that brightened up any room she entered. I liked her right away. When I first met her, she gave me a look that said she wanted to ask me a question.

Finally, one day she did.

"Just how old are you?" she asked.

When I told her I was still in high school, she looked at me with genuine concern. Marcy was always looking out for me, and I appreciated her concern. The following year, Judy moved into the vacant apartment on our floor. She was Marcy's friend, and the three of us quickly became known as the "three musketeers."

The three of us spent hours at the kitchen table drinking tea together, walking to the subway to work, attending parties, and just hanging out. They had no idea that Frank was beating me. To everyone outside my apartment, our lives looked perfect. Frank was the perfect husband.

> This is another of Satan's deceptions. In most violent situations, the husband always presents himself to the outside as a wonderful, loving husband. The abused wife begins to withdraw and becomes depressed. This allows a picture-perfect husband stuck with a depressed wife.

The husband often tells people that he doesn't know what's wrong with his wife. When she finally decides to open up to someone, the seed has already been planted that she has problems, and is a problem. Oftentimes, people feel sorry for the husband. When I finally told people about my abusive situation, many didn't believe me. Frank didn't seem abusive; he had never shown any abusive characteristics.

One day, Marcy and Judy came to the door to ask if I could go out with them. I knew Frank didn't want me to, but he maintained the image of the perfect husband in front of them.

"Go ahead and go," he said. "You need to get out once in a while with your friends."

He is playing with my mind again. He doesn't really want me to go out with friends. Why is he smiling? Looking harder, I could see behind his fake smile all the way to the hatred lurking in his eyes.

My hands trembled as I slipped into jeans and a sweater. *I know he's plotting something, but what?*

"I don't have to go, Frank," I kept saying. "I'll be happy to stay home with you."

"No, you go," he said. "Have fun."

Finally the three of us—the three musketeers—took the subway to the Bronx and had a fantastic time. It felt so good being out with friends that I forgot about all my problems.

When we arrived home, I turned to my friends and told them good night.

I turned my key in the lock, but the door failed to open. *What's wrong with my key?* I knocked on the door.

"Frank, Frank! Are you in there?" He didn't answer. *Where is he? Why won't he let me in?*

I was tired, but had no place to go. I didn't want Marcy and Judy to know he'd locked me out, so I didn't go to them. In the brownstone houses where we lived, the bathrooms are situated outside of the apartments, so I curled up in a corner of the bathroom on top of a stack of towels. I covered myself with one of them.

I planned to be up before my friends, so they would never know what happened. My mind raced. *Surely Frank would wake up, and see*

I was not in the bed. Then he'd come look for me. Or, he would think I stayed out all night. I felt the fear crawling into my mind.

In time, I became drowsy and finally went to sleep. Later, I was awakened by a swift kick in my left side. Frank never said a word, just kicked me and left.

I noticed he left the apartment door open, but I couldn't move without the searing pain in my side making my insides feel like they were on fire. Every time I breathed, waves of pain engulfed me.

Oh Lord, don't let me cry. Frank will hear me, and he'll hurt me again.

I bit my lips until they almost bled, but I didn't utter a sound. The pain was agonizing, but I crawled into the apartment on all fours and pulled myself onto the bed.

I have to keep moving. Maybe I should go to the hospital. No, maybe I better wait to see if the pain eases.

The thoughts of leaving Frank for good ran through my mind. I forced myself out of the bed, even though the pain was worsening.

I struggled to the closet. I held my side gingerly while I began packing my clothes. The pain got so bad, I started sweating, and the room started to tilt. With my head spinning, I gave in and lay back down.

When I woke up, he was standing over me.

"You know I could have killed you," he said. "But I think I'll keep you around. Besides, people might say I was jealous."

He laughed. He picked up my neatly folded clothes, and tossed them all over the room, and then he left.

I sat on the side of the bed with my head in my hands. I couldn't stop crying. The tears made trails down my face and dripped off my chin. Every breath I took made my whole body hurt. I would not give up; I couldn't. I didn't know how, but I had to get through this.

I closed my eyes and began to talk to God.

"God, are you there? Are you listening? I need You, Lord."

I prayed with all my heart that He was listening to me. I knew I'd been out of church awhile, even turned my back on Him. But maybe, just maybe, He would hear my prayers.

I know the devil throws darts at us when we fail to put God first. But I also know that He promises to never leave us nor forsake us. I clung to this—He would never leave me. At one point, I truly believed God had turned His back on me and would never love me again. But I now know that God never said He would stop loving us. He loves us unconditionally. He loves us so much that He gave His only Son to take our place. No one could ever love us like that, especially when we are unlovable, but He does. I thank Him for being the magnificent God that He is. By the time Frank came home, I felt better. Knowing that God had heard my prayer gave me the will to survive.

"Please don't leave, baby," Frank pleaded. "I can't bear the thought of you leaving. I'll get help. I promise. In fact, I know where we can go."

It was just another lie, but I was afraid that if I said anything he would beat me again. I couldn't survive any more of his beatings.

My insides still burned and ached. I knew something was terribly wrong, and I needed medical attention immediately, but I couldn't let him know. He would use my weaknesses against me. So, I waited.

Will I ever get out of this alive? Will he ever let me go? Something, or Someone, urged me to wait.

After Frank left, I called a taxi and went to the emergency room.

When the emergency room doctor asked what happened, I lied. "I fell down the steps," I said.

They believed me, treated me, and sent me home although they felt I should stay overnight for observation.

> Fortunately, today medical personnel are being trained to identify the symptoms of domestic violence and will contact the authorities if there is any question of abuse.

I had mistakenly thought the bleeding was an early menstruation, but it was from the abuse of my body. My insides were traumatized. However, the bleeding had stopped, and I was not in immediate danger.

I looked the doctor square in the eye. "I have to go home. I've got to take care of my family."

Inside, I was shaking. I knew I needed to be home when Frank returned, so he wouldn't hit me again.

The way he operated, he would go into a rage if I went anywhere without telling him. His reasoning to others, and to himself, was that he loved me and was worried.

On the way home, I felt concerned. I hadn't left a note for him and needed to get there before he did.

"Frank, are you home?" I asked as I walked in the door. *Thank God. He's not here.* I walked into an empty apartment and immediately ripped up all the hospital paperwork.

Despite the fact that the doctor told me to get bed rest, I started dinner. I knew I could get it done on time and that would please him. I was safe—for now.

I had to stay away from everyone so no one would see my bruises. Being isolated from my friends and family began to take a toll on me. I missed talking to them and couldn't always use the telephone on the corner. I hadn't told them about the bleeding or how my health was suffering due to the beatings. *I've never kept anything from my family. What if they find out? How will I explain the secrecy?*

Batterers love to isolate the "victim" from their family and friends by saying that they are trying to break them up. If the batterer can isolate the "victim," then they have better control.

I wanted a telephone although Frank had always insisted we didn't need one. Finally, I told him I would pay for the installation and pay the bills. He relented, but it was grudgingly.

The day came when the servicemen appeared at the door. I showed them where to install the phone. Frank stood in the doorway shooting me those looks that could kill. A cold chill began to creep down my back like an ice cube sliding down my spine.

I thought the phone discussion was finished, but I could see he was ready for another battle.

As the men worked, I wanted to scream, "Please don't leave! He's going to kill me!"

To keep them in the house and ensure my safety, I kept asking questions like, "What type of telephone do you recommend?" "Do you think the telephone should go in another place?"

My heart beat so loudly I could almost hear it. I greatly feared what would happen once they left. *What did I do this time? Why is he shooting me looks that could kill?*

In a voice that could freeze a fire, Frank said, "Don't bother the men. Let them work so that they can leave." When they finished, I wanted to leave with them, but I couldn't. Frank stood in the doorway, blocking it with his body, and the men's uneasiness was obvious. They looked from Frank to me, and to each other.

Finally, they said the words I didn't want to hear, "Well, we're finished."

After they walked out, Frank slammed the door. He seemed ten feet tall and growing. His eyes were red. The rage contorted his face, and he grabbed me by my blouse and flung me against the wall like a rag doll.

"You better not use that telephone! You think you're going to tell everyone what's going on, but I've got news for you. I'll know if you use it, because the bill will come here," he said. His voice got louder. "I'll know everyone you talk to. I know a lot more than you think. I can do things that you would never imagine."

He stormed down the stairs and out the door. *Why did he let them install the phone if he won't let me use it?*

After thirty minutes, I was sure Frank was not coming back right away. I prepared to leave. I had to get out of the house.

Just as I got to the door, there he was. I swallowed hard.

The tone of his voice chilled me to the bone. "Get back upstairs, he said." I was still in the hallway, and other people could hear everything that took place. I knew he wouldn't risk that, so I kept going down the stairs, against his will.

Feeling confident, I tried to pass him. When I did, he pushed me. If I hadn't grabbed the railing, I would have fallen. My scream caused our landlord to come out to see what the commotion was about, and Frank told him I tripped.

Like a concerned and loving husband, he held my arm (tighter than necessary) and helped me back upstairs. Inside the apartment, Frank closed the door behind me. Before I could speak a word, he socked me in the jaw. I screamed in pain.

"If you don't shut up, the next one will be your last," he said. As loud as I had screamed, no one came to see if I was all right. The next blow sent my head spinning, and my vision blurred when I tried to make it to the bedroom.

He dogged my steps, yelling obscenities and threats. When I got beside the bed, he ripped my clothes, threw me on the bed, and got on top of me. He raped me repeatedly, until I just wanted to die.

Later in the shower I scrubbed myself, trying to remove the dirty feeling. I cried so hard I could barely see what I was doing. No matter how much soap and water I used, I couldn't make the filth go away.

I was tired, and I didn't have any more fight left in me. For the first time in my life, I wanted God to take me. I wanted to die.

Why was I still alive in this hell? Why, God? Don't You care? Why didn't You strike him dead?

Why indeed; I didn't know then that I was being prepared for my ministry helping others who are abused. As odd as this may sound, I know God spared my life to tell this story to help my sisters and, yes, brothers, and I will not fail Him.

Chapter IV

I woke to the sound of loud music. Frank was playing records and dancing by himself, which seemed strange. *Now what?* I began getting ready for work, anxious to get out of his way. He was in a good mood, and I didn't want to change anything. He didn't have to be at work until afternoon and maybe that's why he was so happy. Whatever it was, I wanted to get out as soon as I could. He could change at any moment. How could he be so happy after what he'd done to me?

He sat at the table reading the paper and said, "I think I'll work overtime, so we can have some extra money." *Huh?*

I was in disbelief. The events of the previous night seemed to have been completely wiped from his mind. He acted as if we were the happiest couple in the world, which was what most people thought anyway. Since he still had time before getting ready for work, he decided to walk me to the train station.

He noticed I was limping. He asked me why, but I didn't want to discuss it. Whenever I complained about pain, he became enraged as though it was something I could control. He wouldn't leave the subject alone, so I told him I was having some pain in my side and would probably see the doctor. I worked in a hospital, so it would be no problem.

While on the subway, the pain intensified, and it felt as though someone had stuck a knife in my side and twisted it. A nice, older man offered me his seat. *Something is very wrong.* Numbness crept up the lower part of my body.

The doctor had said I had some internal bleeding, but in the emergency room, it had miraculously stopped. By the time I arrived at work, I could barely move.

My employer called me into his office and asked me what was wrong. I broke down and, in tears, told him my little "secret." For a moment, releasing the mental pain was wonderful. A great weight lifted from my shoulders.

What was I thinking when I opened up? That he would provide me with safety?

I watched my boss's face turn from concern into a scowl. "Frank's your husband! I don't want any part of this," he said. "And one more thing, it would probably be wise not to discuss this with anyone else. You don't want anyone else to get hurt." I left his office with additional pain—the pain of knowing no one cared.

My physical pain persisted, and I once again went to the emergency room. I talked to another doctor and learned that I had additional damage to my insides from the previous rapes. I was afraid to say anything.

Nobody believes me. Why should I open myself to that pain again?

I looked at the doctor and said, "My husband's rough when we make love." I hoped the doctor would give me some painkillers and send me home.

Instead, the young doctor didn't believe me.

"Now, tell me again," he said, "what happened?"

I refused to tell him.

"If you want to talk about it, you can call me. I'll keep it confidential."

Yeah, right. I can't trust anyone.

I'd tried to confide in my boss, but it backfired. I wasn't taking any more chances.

What if Frank got wind of it? Would he hurt the doctor? As for my family, he had orchestrated it so that no one would believe me. Besides, I was afraid to tell them. How could I live with myself knowing I had caused them trouble? Frank had everything figured out. It's a wonder

I didn't lose my mind, but in my heart I knew God kept me safe and protected me.

Sometimes, I thought wild thoughts. What if I could be a "good, obedient wife"? Maybe then I could keep the peace in my home. Even if he beat me once in awhile, I could survive it as long as he left my family alone. *What else could I do?*

Although I was young, I reasoned that I could learn from others what it meant to be the type of wife Frank wanted and needed. Once I learned the tricks to a good marriage, my own marriage would work, and he would stop hitting me. Eventually, all this would be behind me, and we would never mention it again. We'd continue to be the fun-loving couple everyone thought we were.

Christmas came and went and the new year roared in like a lion. We were invited to a party in Manhattan for New Year's Eve, and I felt excited. I would see friends that I hadn't seen in awhile as well as some of my family. It would be wonderful to sit and laugh with them.

"You don't look so happy," one of my cousins said a few weeks before. After that remark, I planned to make everyone think that nothing was wrong.

What would happen to me if Frank knew they were suspicious? I determined to make them think that we still had a perfect marriage.

Frank was in one of his good moods when he came home that evening with a dress he wanted me to wear. I later found out that not only had he gotten it from a factory where his brother worked, but my sister-in-law got the same dress.

He seemed pleased that I planned to wear the dress even though it wasn't something I liked. When I finished dressing and put on some lipstick, I turned to ask him how I looked.

"I've told you before you don't need lipstick! It makes you look cheap. Take it off!" Obediently and without question, I wiped the lipstick off. That pacified him. He smiled.

"Too bad we're going out. We could have our own party. Girl, you look good!"

I smiled at the compliment. It was New Year's Eve, and things were beginning to look up. Maybe this would be a good year; a year of change.

The party turned out great. Frank and I danced most of the night, and once more our friends started calling us lovebirds.

Frank was attentive. He brought me some hors d'oeuvres, making sure I had enough to eat and was comfortable. He didn't leave my side, and when he saw me talking to someone else, he stood close enough to eavesdrop.

My friends only saw him as a loving husband, but I knew he was making sure I didn't tell anyone about our home life. He was so thoughtful that some of the wives said their husbands could learn lessons from Frank.

As the evening progressed, Frank did a turnabout and began dancing with almost every woman there. I too began dancing with a couple of our friends. Then I saw a familiar look steal across his face. The old rage was still there, boiling just beneath the surface.

I quit dancing immediately and sat down. I watched his facial gestures noting that he was upset because I'd danced with friends. *Why is it all right for him to socialize and have fun, but not me?*

We'd known these couples forever. They were our friends. I felt no attraction to any of them. But Frank made it plain. I was not there to have fun; I was there to make an appearance and be a devoted, caring wife.

"It's almost midnight!" the announcer said. "Put on your hats and grab your horns so we can welcome in the New Year!"

I put on my hat and picked up a horn. Frank's mood seemed to have changed because he embraced, and then kissed me. "Happy New Year!" he shouted above the din of noise around us. "I love you."

After the party ended, we headed toward the subway. It was a long walk, and I made a comment that I wished we had accepted a ride from one of our friends. His look made me wince.

While we waited for the train, Frank turned to me. "You thought you were so smart tonight, dancing with all the men, and acting like I wasn't there. You embarrassed me and yourself."

"I'm too tired to argue, Frank." I turned around to sit down on a nearby subway bench. The next thing I knew he'd punched the side of my head.

"Don't you know I love you?" he yelled. "How could you treat me like that?" He punched me again. This time it was so hard, I hit the ground. Powerful ringing sounded in my ears, and the dizziness blurred my vision.

I was so out of it that I didn't realize a crowd had formed until I heard an older man say, "Someone should help her." Others said they didn't want to get involved.

"She'll probably tell us to mind our own business," said one woman. "Women like her don't want help. They like getting beat. It's women like her that make it hard for other women."

So no one helped me. Again, I was alone. I tried to fight back, but he was too strong. Frank just kept punching me until I collapsed again. Every time I tried to stand, he'd push me back down. *Why doesn't the ground just open up and swallow me? How can these people stand here watching? He's going to kill me, and no one cares.*

When the train finally came, Frank had to practically carry me to the seat. I felt people staring at me, but I couldn't look up. I felt too ashamed. *It's a brand-new year, and nothing has changed.*

It didn't bother him to fight in public. He kept saying that no one would help me because I was ugly, stupid, and weak. Too powerless to protest, I listened to his ranting all the way home.

We walked from the subway station, and he didn't seem in the least concerned that I was in pain, and my head was still swimming from the punches. He just kept yelling, "Hurry up!" When someone turned around, he acted as though I'd had too much to drink. He played the part of the wounded husband stuck with a drunken wife, and the pitiful look on his face made it seem true.

A passerby shook his head, looking at me with disgust. Then he gave Frank a sympathetic look that said, "I'm so sorry," and kept moving. *Sorry? Can't you see I'm hurt?* I finally arrived home and crawled into bed.

I was horrified at what had happened—again. *Maybe if I'm lucky, I'll die in my sleep. Is this the way the year will turn out?* Was the old wives' tale true? Would whatever happened on New Year's Eve repeat itself all year long?

CHAPTER V

Today was the block party. Our street would be closed all day so we could have an outdoor party. Every house on the block would contribute something. There would be clowns for the children, a Ferris wheel, and ponies would be arriving later in the day. We had been planning the event for months, and the day had finally arrived.

The police made announcements that everyone would have to move their cars so the street could be closed. It was 7:00 a.m. on a beautiful summer morning, and we had a lot to do before ten o'clock when the block party officially began.

The police announcement woke me up, and I started to get ready. But Frank grabbed my shoulder and asked me where I was going.

I smiled and said, "Don't you remember, honey? Today is the block party, and I'm going to help them prepare the food and get things ready. I'm on the committee."

His friendly voice turned into a low growl. "You aren't going anywhere. You better get back in bed and perform your wifely duties. That's all you're good for."

I thought he was kidding. He couldn't possibly mean what he said. I did everything I could to keep him happy, because when he was happy, he wouldn't fight with me. In the back of my mind, I still held onto the dream that one day he would just leave me, and I would be free to live again. *Why was he still here? He hated me.* Maybe his plan was to beat me to death or maybe just drive me insane.

Suddenly he grabbed me, digging his nails into my arm and snapping me back to reality. "Did you hear what I said? I said get back in the bed!"

He ordered me to take my clothes off. Instead I walked away. I should have known better. Whenever I walked away from him, he got angrier. He grabbed me again and ripped my gown off, leaving me standing there naked and afraid.

When he grabbed me and threw me down, I thought, *This is rape! He's my husband, but this is rape!* I begged him to stop, but that made him angrier.

He slapped my face, and with one hand around my throat, proceeded to continue his assault. I felt as if I was being ripped apart, and I felt helpless to stop it.

If God is merciful, why is He allowing this? After the onslaught, I lay on the bed in disarray. I couldn't move. I could barely think.

He reached inside the closet and pulled out the gun. "See, I still have it. Tell somebody about this, and you die! Now you can go help them prepare for the block party. I'll be watching you from the window, and I'll know everyone you talk to. There is nothing you can do because they will die if they try to help. So go ahead and enjoy yourself!" he said, and then laughed.

I don't know why I believed he could do such a thing, but I did. I was terrified, and I didn't want anyone else harmed. I decided I would help with preparation, but I wouldn't talk to anyone. I showered, put on my clothes and started downstairs. His cruel laughter rang in my ears for hours.

Downstairs, I walked and acted like a zombie. I didn't know what to do. It would be very easy to just cut and run, but suppose he was serious about hurting my family and friends?

I threw myself into helping my neighbors prepare for the party. Pretty soon I forgot that I wasn't going to talk and began to smile and even laugh again. As I walked farther down the block, I noticed that Frank came outside and sat down on the brownstone's steps. When I walked over to him, he gave me a look that made my blood run ice cold. My neighbor saw the look.

"Why don't you come inside to talk?" she asked. I made up every excuse why I couldn't go inside. She looked into my eyes, frowned, and handed me a case of glasses. Then she said loud enough for Frank to hear, "I need you to help me wash these glasses." I didn't even turn around to look at him.

Inside her house, I fell against the wall, almost dropping the case of glasses. I began to cry hysterically. When I finally calmed down, I told her what had happened. She said I could stay with her, but I knew that would only make things worse. She didn't know what he was capable of, and I didn't want her to be hurt.

Someone came to the door and said Frank wanted me to come home. *This is going to cost me. He knows what we are talking about.* My neighbor tried to keep me safe by saying I didn't have to go. But even more, I wanted to keep her safe.

I walked down the steps, trembling in fear. When I walked outside, Frank asked me where I'd been.

"Just helping with the food and washing glasses," I said. He grabbed my arm with uncompromising strength. No one saw how tightly he grasped me. My neighbors let us pass, while trying to convince us to stay a little longer. He practically dragged me up the stairs, and when we got inside, he pushed me against the wall so hard, I hit my head.

About the same time, the phone rang. It was my neighbor.

She lowered her voice, "Should I call the police?"

"Yes," I answered. I could hear her husband in the background telling her to mind her business, but she said she was calling anyway.

Frank snatched the telephone out of my hand and slammed the receiver down. He began slapping me across the face, saying repeatedly that I deserved it. I ran to the window and screamed, hoping someone would come to my rescue. No one came, but I had gotten their attention.

When Frank pulled me away from the window, I noticed that the block party quieted down. Everyone on the street that day was looking up at our window. The looks of terror were evident as Frank slammed the window shut. He was so angry he didn't notice that others were watching. *The secret is out. He can't threaten me anymore. People know what is happening.*

I tried to fight back hoping that maybe this time I would hurt him. But he grabbed my arm, twisting it behind my back and threatening to break my arm. He slapped me again, and then stormed out of the house saying he was going to work.

I don't know if anyone said anything to him about the incident, but I knew he would think of something to say. He was getting better with his lies. He always smiled around other people, making it seem as if I were the crazy one. After all, as he constantly told me, everything was my fault. *Maybe it is my fault. Maybe I am crazy.*

Not long after he left, the police arrived. I told them what happened, and they said that since he was my husband I couldn't press charges. It was considered a "domestic dispute." However, they said they would talk to him and try to calm him down.

> Thankfully, this is no longer the case. Now, when a woman is being abused by her husband, it is treated as a criminal act, and the abuser can be arrested. In the 1970s, there were no victim service agencies or shelters for abused women. Spouses could not press charges because the law felt that whatever occurred between a husband and wife was none of their business. The police would come to the house, take the husband outside and talk to him and then send him back inside. That only made matters worse. So, many cases of domestic violence went unreported.

When I walked the police to the door, I noticed my neighbors still stood outside; some shook their heads in disbelief, while others looked shocked.

I felt both embarrassed and ashamed by what had happened. I wanted to sink into the ground and disappear. As the shock wore off, some of my neighbors wanted to know how to help.

They even offered to take me to the hospital, but I was terrified. If I went to the hospital, Frank would be furious. Of course, he would not show that side of him; he would play the part of the concerned husband, telling them that I was out of control and he was only trying to quiet me.

I knew things would be worse if I needed to be admitted to the hospital. It would be an inconvenience for him. I knew I would have to tell them what really happened, and no one would do anything. I would only hear the same old things I'd heard so often, "Try to work things out." So I chose not to go.

God, why is this happening to me? What have I done that is so terrible that I have to suffer like this? Have you forgotten me? Don't you even care what happens to me? Why won't you answer? Why do you allow him to continue to hurt me? Hello, God?

Those thoughts raced through my mind that day, but somehow I knew God was watching. I knew He had not left me, and no matter what happened to me, I would never deny Him.

But why wouldn't He speak to me?

The one person I could turn to when in trouble was my Uncle Ernest who was now very ill. He was like a father to me, and he was the one person in the world I felt safe to confide in.

He was in the hospital in early 1970, and I made up my mind to go see him every day. Surprisingly, Frank didn't try to stop me. Ernest couldn't talk without holding his finger over an opening in his throat where he'd had a tracheotomy, a procedure where a tube was inserted so he could breathe.

Ernest was a very proud and God-fearing man who, from the time I was a young child, always told me that God loved me very much.

"No matter what you go through, child, all you have to do is talk to God about it," he said. Then he would read Scripture to me and explain each passage.

During my terrible ordeal, I tried to remember some of the things he taught me, but they seemed locked away in my memory, and just out of my reach. Ernest was such a good man, and I never dreamed God would take him away from me. If he wasn't around to give me wise advice, I felt as if I would lose every bit of hope. Ernest was my one special link to God because of his closeness with the Lord.

I looked at Ernest lying in the hospital bed. He was so ill, and he looked so frail. I knew he very well might die. I watched Ernest fight to live. It was hard for him to be helpless. He was so frustrated that he would cry because he could not articulate what he wanted to say. It broke my heart to see him like that. *Lord, I know I'm being selfish, but please don't take my uncle from me. I need him more than You do.*

Frank and I would bring Ernest a pen and paper every day so he could write down what he wanted to verbalize. Once, when I went to his bedside without Frank, Ernest wanted to know what was wrong.

"I know you're not happy," he mouthed. I wanted to tell him what was wrong, but I couldn't. He continued to insist there must be something wrong. I only wanted Ernest to get better, not to tell him my problems.

Frank understood how sick Ernest was, and I couldn't trust Frank around him. I was afraid he'd somehow let Ernest know how bad things were between us.

Frank would shoot me a mean look whenever I spoke quietly to my uncle, and then he would look at him and whisper, "*You better not say a thing.*" I'd been with Frank so long I could almost read his mind.

I kept quiet, but sank deeper and deeper into my well-worn shell of depression. I had never lied to my uncle about anything, and it hurt me that we couldn't have one of our talks. It filled me with guilt that I wasn't being honest, but again I felt I was keeping him alive longer by being quiet.

Ernest, I know you'd know what to do.

Even my aunt began to ask what was wrong. Both she and my mother were talking about my situation, I knew, because they asked me the same questions. I felt I had to protect them at any cost and pretty soon my shell became a brick wall that no one could penetrate.

The wall stopped questions from being asked, and it kept my emotions from leaking out. I was becoming hidden in my empty shell, surrounded by a wall of fear and low self-esteem.

I didn't trust Frank, and for sure, didn't know how far he would go with his threats, but I knew better than to take too many chances. I was always afraid he'd hurt my family. My thoughts wandered wildly.

Maybe I could find them a place to stay; somewhere so Frank couldn't find them. But how could I get them to leave? They would think I was full-blown crazy. Maybe I could protect them. But how? Why did I feel so responsible for their safety?

One day while visiting my uncle in the hospital, he grabbed my hand and held it tightly. With his eyes, he begged me to tell him what was wrong.

"I'm fine, Ernest," I lied. *Forgive me. I can't tell you.*

Finally, he stopped asking. By his expression I could tell he was not convinced, and he was hurt because I wouldn't open up. I blamed Frank for destroying the closeness I had with my uncle.

Later that week, Ernest wrote a note to my mom saying he wanted to see Frank. The words of that note sent chills racing through my body. I decided to go with Frank for the visit. I was terrified Ernest was going to question Frank, but he just wanted to say he was selling us his car.

Transportation at last. I was thrilled to know we would have a car, but I didn't know that it meant I would hardly see Frank. After we acquired the car, Frank disappeared for days at a time. After awhile, I noticed a great deal of mileage on the car, and I believed Frank was sometimes leaving the state. My uncle never knew what was going on between Frank and me, and I think he would have been deeply hurt had he known.

I knew Ernest was trying to make life easier for me by providing us with transportation, but Frank used the car to run around with his old "friends." Knowing my uncle stood up for his belief in God, Frank showed complete disrespect by using what was meant to help me for his own pleasure.

After Ernest died, I felt certain he would watch over me from heaven. In a way, I felt he would be a guardian angel. I hoped Frank would know that God stayed near me and would hesitate treating me like he had in the past.

Ernest had a special relationship with God, and I remember that whenever I spoke with him I felt safe, believing nothing could ever happen to me. Now that he was gone, I had the feeling that he would always be with me, see what I was going through, understand my silence, and forgive me.

When I married, I stopped going to church. That was the worst mistake I ever made. Even after all these years, I realize Uncle Ernest never stopped praying for me, and I thank God for him. There are so many people alive today because of prayers. I remember when church people talked about praying grandparents, relatives, and friends who never gave up on an individual, no matter what. We should all be thankful for those saints.

It has been more than twenty-five years since Ernest's death, and when I think of him, I have nothing but loving memories. He would be proud to know I've dedicated my life to the Lord. As close as he was to God, he probably knew it would happen some day.

If he had said I someday would be a minister, I probably would have laughed. That was the last thing on my mind. I was having too much fun. Ministry did not fit into my plans.

CHAPTER VI

I awoke early. It was the middle of the summer and the previous night had been so humid, I could hardly sleep. I'd moved into the living room to sleep on the couch where a cool breeze blew in from the backyard. When I walked into the bedroom that morning, I noticed Frank had not come home the previous night. Last night, I'd watched him pack a duffle bag.

I questioned him as he packed, and he said, "Don't you worry; this belongs to one of my friends. He needs some clothes because he ran into some bad luck. I'll just give this to him and be back within a half hour." I followed him out to the car and watched as he tossed the bag into the car and drove off.

The cool morning air felt good as it wafted through the open windows. *Is he gone for good?* I breathed a small sigh of relief. Part of me was glad he had left, but another part worried that something might have happened to him. After several hours, I was afraid that maybe something really had happened. I called the police.

"Ma'am," a gruff voice said, "a person has to be missing twenty-four hours before we can investigate."

To relieve my worried mind, I began cooking bacon. I hoped Frank hadn't gotten into an accident, because I didn't think I could handle it. I would be forced to care for him, and I couldn't trust myself. After everything he'd done to me, I was afraid I might hurt him, or just let him suffer. Before I finished scrambling eggs, I heard his footsteps coming up the stairs. When he walked in, I felt both relieved and angry.

"Where've you been, Frank?" I asked.

The menacing look told me loud and clear that I shouldn't have questioned him.

"You probably think I was with another woman, don't you?" Before I could answer, he stormed toward the door. I later learned he *had* been with someone else. He figured I didn't have sense enough to figure it out.

For a second, I thought he was leaving me, and I didn't want him to go. What happened next took me by surprise. I ran behind him and the words just tumbled out.

"Please don't leave. I was just worried about you. Forgive me."

What am I doing? I can't believe I asked forgiveness. I am not some wimpy woman. I can make it on my own. Why did I beg him to stay after all he's done to me? Am I crazy?

"You should be glad I want you because nobody else does," he said. "Besides, you're not smart enough to live by yourself."

My mind began playing tricks on me. Soon I began to believe he was right. *I will probably lose my apartment and my job, because I'm not smart enough. Like Frank keeps saying, my friends will laugh at me. They'll all abandon me.*

Every word he said cut into my soul like lashes from a whip, and I felt as if he had beaten me again. This time, though, it was a deeper pain, and it remained longer than a beating, creating a bruised spot in my very spirit. Frank had found still another way to hurt me. He seemed to enjoy the mental abuse. He was amused, watching the tears slide down my face.

This way, the only marks he left on me would be invisible, but the pain remained inside of me and festered. This kind of pain was so immense that I sometimes felt like balling up into a fetal position.

His words pounded in my brain. *Nobody else wants me. I'm useless. I can't even take care of myself. Am I going insane?*

The mental abuse was far worse than the physical. At least there was an end to the physical abuse. I learned the hard way that mental abuse was a good way to drive someone crazy.

After Frank realized he could hurt me without touching me, he began staying out longer. When he came home, if I said anything or even looked at him strange, it initiated a fight. Then, the strangest thing happened; he changed.

One night he had been his usual mean self and the next morning, he woke up as someone different. All of a sudden, he couldn't do enough for me. I became suspicious and refused to turn my back on him. As far as I knew, he would come home one night sweet as anything, and then change again, usually for the worst. I had witnessed his mood swings before.

What could he be up to now? What else could he do to me? I know what a turkey feels like right before Thanksgiving. The farmer fattens the turkey up with the best grain, knowing his evil plans for him. All the while, the turkey begins to trust the farmer because he is being nice, and the turkey doesn't attempt to run away. Then, when it is least expected, the farmer gets ready to do him in.

For now, though, Frank was a loving husband. If I needed anything, he was right there. He stayed home and worked harder than ever, so I could have anything I wanted. What was most surprising, we never argued. We even began to talk about our marriage, which was something we'd never done before.

One evening, we sat on the sofa watching TV and Frank said, "I don't know why I treat you like I do." He grabbed a handful of popcorn, and then added, "Maybe we should go to counseling."

He shocked me by calling his family and telling them I was a good wife, and that he expected too much of me. "I'm just a perfectionist," he told them.

I was thrilled that our lives seemed changed. *Maybe he means it this time.* We began going out to dances and the movies again. Our good friends resumed calling us "lovebirds." Finally, everything was going fine. I began to feel like a wife again, and my home became a place I loved.

Friends and family began saying that I was like myself again. I was happy, and I conveniently forgot about God. After all, He knew my heart. Besides, God is everywhere; I didn't need church. I could pray at home.

Frank again became the most important thing in my life, and I felt I should stay home on Sunday with him. He didn't care about church, and I didn't want to take chances and mess up our new, wonderful relationship.

Why is it when we want to drop something from our lives, it is usually God? We convince ourselves that Sunday is our only day to relax, and we stop going to church. We don't go to Bible study because it's the middle of the week and we're tired, but if someone comes up with free tickets to a play or restaurant, our energy returns.

I knew God was supposed to be my "first love," but so many times I relegated him to second place. Unknowingly, I put Frank ahead of God, and in so doing; I made Frank an idol—something God detests. I wanted to believe that God was happy that our marriage was working. I never considered that He should come first. I guess I was selfish. I always thought of my needs first—like wanting a child. Oh, how I wanted a child.

CHAPTER VII

I loved children, and I asked the Lord to give me a houseful of them. In fact, my wildest dream was to have at least eight children. I wanted to see laughing, crawling, playful children all over the place.

Every month I prayed for a child. I once cried out loud to God, "Lord, if you give me a child, I will raise him or her for you. It would really be Your child. I want this more than anything else."

I identified with Hannah in the Bible. When the Lord gave her Samuel, I know just how she felt. She too promised to give her child, Samuel, back to God. Although I wasn't even attending church, I meant every word. A child would be a miracle in my life, and I promised that he or she would be in church every Sunday. I wanted them to know God, and that He was always with them.

Not too long afterward, I thought I might be pregnant. I was filled with wonderment that it could even be possible. I hesitated visiting the doctor, because I didn't want to be disappointed.

But a couple of weeks later, I developed a terrible cold and my first thought was that I had the flu. I went to a nearby doctor's office. After I spoke to him about possibly being pregnant, he suggested I see an obstetrician, which increased my excitement.

It has been more than thirty years now, and I still remember the freshness of the day the doctor smiled at me and said, "You are definitely pregnant."

She gave me vitamins, instructions, and a prenatal appointment. Finally, things were happening the way I envisioned them. In spite of my own disobedience in not attending church, God blessed me with a growing child. *Thank you, God that you didn't give up on me.* I couldn't stop thanking God, and I remembered my promise—this child would be returned to Him.

I wanted to be a mother more than anything, and I determined I would be the best mother possible. This child would be loved so much. I gently placed my hands on my stomach and said, "I can't wait to see you. You are beautiful. I love you already."

My mother and aunt were thrilled when I told them, and they both screamed. My mother would have the grandchild she was waiting for, and my aunt would have a great-great niece or nephew. I called my father, and he said, "It's about time. I've been waiting long enough."

I couldn't wait to tell Frank he would be a father. As soon as he walked in the door, I walked up to him. Tears spilled down my cheeks as I told him the good news. He was so happy that he cried too. He called both his sister and brother, and I could hear their excitement coming through the phone.

That night I lay awake thinking of the new life beginning inside me. How I wanted to hold my baby. When I finally fell asleep, I dreamed of the baby. The next day, I couldn't take my thoughts off the new child growing inside.

I am so happy, Lord. Thank you for this new life You gave me.

For hours, I would talk to her and sing songs I had learned years ago in church.

It's raining today, sweet baby. Do you hear that? That loud sound is thunder, but don't you worry, you're safe and warm right under Mama's heart. Oh, thank You, Lord, for this blessing!

I worked as close as possible to my delivery date, so I could buy everything I needed for my child. At the time, I was working for a bank and that meant standing on my feet—a lot. The baby was due in August, and I intended to work through July. Summers in New York can be brutal at times, but I was young and eager to work. One day while waiting for the bus, I felt unusually tired. I began questioning my motives for working. Although it was spring, it was already hot and humid.

When I arrived at work that day, I had a strange feeling that I should stop working immediately. Just quit. I had originally told my employer I would be starting maternity leave in three weeks. However, after the first week, I had a sick feeling growling in my stomach every day, and I knew I couldn't make it. I quit the following week. It wasn't part of our plan, but I was thankful that Frank understood.

"We'll manage," he said.

When my parting day arrived, my coworkers gave me a baby shower, which added to my excitement. Spread before me were tiny articles of baby clothes, cloth diapers and bottles. I couldn't help myself—I was so thankful for all the love and care that I cried.

God, why are you blessing me so much? I don't deserve all of this. Thank you.

When I left the job, I was eager to become a mother and housewife; two new professions. At first, I was happy to be home. I slept late, and Frank prepared my breakfast before he left for work. He had been even more attentive since I became pregnant. The fighting had stopped, and we were both excited about becoming parents. I knew I'd made the right choice to leave my job.

On the very day I originally should have left my job, breaking news interrupted my TV programming—a bank robbery occurred in the bank where I'd worked. To my shock, the security guard was killed.

In my heart, I know it was the Holy Spirit who told me to quit two weeks earlier. He loved me enough to move my unborn child and me out of danger, and I know He will protect us from all other harm. Despite knowing God's hand rested upon my baby and me that day, I still didn't go back to church.

My excuse was that I was tired. Not only that, church took too long.

God will understand. I'm eight months pregnant, and my back aches all the time. Church just takes too much time; besides I don't know how I would ever get comfortable on those hard pews.

I began to prepare for my baby's birth. I went window-shopping, and walked through the infant department at department stores. It felt as if the abuse in my married life was only a bad memory. Frank had made a complete change in personality, and he was more loving and attentive than ever.

Some days, he would be so excited that he would rub my growing abdomen and laugh. Sometimes he came home early from work just to talk about the baby. Nothing made him angry anymore. In fact, sometimes when I'd feel cranky, he would laugh at me, saying I should calm down because he didn't want his child to be angry. He often said he wanted his baby to be happy, just like we were. He smiled and laughed at everything. Frank was beginning to be one of the happiest persons I knew.

As we rejoiced about the upcoming birth, we received news that my mother-in-law in North Carolina was in a serious accident. Since I wasn't working, I went to see her, along with my sister and brother-in-law. I was a little more than eight months pregnant and in good health.

I knew I could rest there, and that the baby would be fine. After all, my baby was dedicated to God.

I had only been at my mother-in-law's house for a few days, when she took a turn for the worse. We were shocked because we all thought she was doing so well. She was excited about my baby; and she was looking forward to becoming a grandmother again. Not long after our conversation, she died. I was upset that she would not be alive to see the grandchild she wanted so much. She had made so many plans for the baby. And we had talked at length about how she looked forward to holding the baby in her arms.

I was standing right beside my mother-in-law when she took her last breath. Chills pulsated through my body, and I began to cramp. In a few minutes, I doubled over in pain.

Immediately, the family rushed me to the hospital. After a few hours, we realized it was only false labor. I then moved in with one of Frank's family members for a short while. I had nowhere else to go, and something about her insistent offer that I stay with her until Frank arrived made me suspicious.

I was traumatized seeing my mother-in-law die right in front of me, and the doctor gave me some tranquilizers. I was told to take one every six hours, as needed. But a family member wanted me to take a tablet every hour. I wanted to believe she hadn't heard the doctor right. I didn't know what was going on, but regardless, I didn't take the pills.

Every time she came into the room, my eyes popped open. Something about that room troubled me and reminded me of times in New York when Frank and I were having problems.

I had to remember I was in North Carolina, not Brooklyn, but the tension in the air felt familiar, and I knew that whatever it was, it wanted to harm both my baby and me.

With sudden clarity I knew that there was a battle raging over my soul, and my baby's soul. The devil didn't want us to survive, and he was doing his utmost to prevent it. But God had plans for my child. He had already claimed this unborn child as His. "Before I formed you in the womb I knew you, and before you were born I consecrated you: I appointed you a prophet to the nations" (Jer. 1:5, NRSV).

Because of being eight months pregnant and traumatized by my mother-in-law's death, I wasn't allowed to attend her funeral. I stayed at the house, where I became more and more uncomfortable. Finally, I became so uneasy that I knew it was time to go home. I was ready for Frank to come get me.

I wanted to be home with my family in familiar surroundings. I wanted to make sure my baby was safe, and I knew once I was home, everything would be good. When Frank and I returned to Brooklyn, Frank's personality began to change, and he showed erratic symptoms again. I wanted to believe he was reacting to the death of his mother. He became distant and didn't come home when he usually did. I began to see a visible change in him. Fear welled up in my chest, and I became frightened.

Is the abuse beginning again? Can't I make dinner, do laundry, and pack the baby's clothes for the hospital without feeling this overwhelming fear?

For the last few months of my pregnancy, Frank had been the picture of a doting husband and father. I refused to believe he would revert to his old ways. Time was drawing near for the birth of our baby, and I was feeling more than a little anxious.

Long ago, I had made up my mind that Frank would never hurt my child. However, his mood swings began to appear more often, and I determined to stay out of his way. I thought he would never hit me because of the pregnancy, but now with his behavior changing so often and sometimes so radically, I wasn't sure. Maybe he was afraid of the prospects of becoming a father. It didn't matter; to be safe I stayed out of his way as much as possible. I tried to have his dinner ready on time, and if he didn't feel like talking, I quietly retreated to another room. I did everything in my power not to upset him.

My due date came closer, and I knew I had to pre-register at the hospital. Frank didn't want to take the time to do the prescribed registration because he didn't feel it was important.

Pacing the floor one day, he threw out rapid-fire questions: "Well, what would they do if you went into labor? Throw you out in the street? Would they?" he demanded. To avoid making him angry, I went without him to get my papers in order.

"Frank," I said one evening after supper, "here's the money to pay the hospital bill." I put the money on the table, and then kicked off my shoes, held onto the sides of my large belly and eased into a chair.

Frank stormed into the apartment later that night slamming the door and looking frantic. It was evident that he'd been thinking about the money. "OK," he said angrily, "where'd you get it?"

I stammered. "I-I saved it, Frank. I needed to buy some things for the baby."

"You've been holding out on me, haven't you? Where'd you get it? Where's the rest of it?"

Then he slapped me across the face. I felt the burn all the way into my jawline. I put my hand to my face in disbelief, and then tears coursed down my cheeks.

He hit me! I am pregnant with his child, and Frank slapped me! I will not let my baby go through this. I will leave first. He seemed to read my mind.

"Where would you go? You're pregnant, remember? You can't live with your mother because there's no room. Besides if you ever leave me, I'll just take the baby, and you'll never see us again." A smirk settled on his face.

I believed every word he said and I stayed—despite what I felt. The Devil knows exactly what to say to us. He knows which buttons to push because he knows our weaknesses. Mine was that I felt I could not raise a child myself. I was convinced Frank was right. Where would I go? I couldn't go to my mother with a newborn baby. She had no room for two more people. I was twenty-one years old, and had never been around many babies. In those days, twenty-one was very young to be married, but pregnant? *What can I do?* I was convinced God wasn't listening to my plea, and I had no place to go.

Angry thoughts raced through my mind. *What kind of person hits a pregnant woman? I can't leave if I wanted to. I am stuck.* If I left, he'd said he would take my child. He might even become angry enough to seriously hurt me, possibly even kill me. If I was not alive and my baby lived, what would happen? He would never let my family take care of the baby.

If I did leave, I was convinced that Frank would eventually find us. I knew Frank would refuse to let me take anything with me. *How could I raise a child alone?* I didn't have a job, no babysitter and knew nothing about raising children.

I'm trapped. I will never be free from my husband. Where can I turn? There's no place to go. Frank would never leave. I was having his child, and even if I left, he would find us, take the baby and leave the state, maybe even the country.

As suddenly as the abuse started, it stopped. Frank became an attentive husband again. *Maybe he's grieving for his mother.*

Later, Frank seemed genuinely sorry when he said, "I'm sorry, baby, I can't believe I hit you." He vowed he would never touch me again. If he did, he wanted me to leave and take the baby because he didn't deserve to live. I agreed with him, especially the part about his "not deserving to live." I hoped he died right there on the spot. I had no feelings for him anymore, so why didn't I leave?

I wanted so much to believe he wanted the baby and was ready to calm down and start a family. Besides, this time, he promised he would let me go if he ever hit me again. What I didn't realize was that although he said he would not hit me, he had also said that *if* he hit me again, I could leave. He couldn't even trust himself not to strike me.

My due date was fast arriving. I couldn't wait to meet the little one whose elbows and knees continually poked me—day and night.

Finally, the day came for my baby to arrive. It had begun as just another day. I had been restless the previous night and kept waking up. My stomach cramped, then the cramps would disappear. It was hot and muggy with no breeze. The fan was blowing hot air, and I was miserable.

Frank wasn't home, and I had become frightened by the pain. I called my mother to spend the night with me. It had been a long night.

But, today turned out to be the most exciting day of my life. It was one of the hottest days in July. In fact, the whole month was hotter than usual. Every day the temperature registered 98 degrees or above.

I was thrilled the baby was almost here, because I couldn't wait to hold him or her. The extra baby weight made my pregnancy that much more uncomfortable, especially in the unrelenting heat of that New York summer.

As my back pains intensified, I told my mother that maybe if I rested, the pain would go away. She said she was going home and would keep calling to make sure I was all right. Then, it happened…my water broke! I was glad Frank had gotten home in time.

My mother excitedly told him that we needed to get to the hospital. On the way down the stairs, Frank reached over and took my hand, and he smiled. *Maybe he is changing. After all, he'll be a father soon.*

As soon as we entered the hospital, a pain shuddered through me. I held my hands beneath my belly.

The nurse looked at me. "Do you have your reservation papers?"

"Frank, did you get the papers?" My husband purposely walked ahead of me. "Frank?"

The nurse took me to see the hospital's counselor. "I'm sorry, but you don't have a reservation. No one paid your deposit."

Another pain coursed through me. *Of course it was paid. Frank paid it.* Then the realization came that Frank had not paid my bill. *Where will I go? What did Frank do with the money?*

Frank made excuses, and my doctor said that without the paid reservation there was nothing she could do.

I nearly went berserk. *What will happen to me? Where will I have my baby? Will I have to go back home and have it there?*

I lumbered into the waiting room. Frank's jaw was set, and I knew he was getting angry. *The nerve of him! Why is he angry? He's not the one in labor!*

For several months, he knew he hadn't paid for my reservation. First, I was angry with Frank because of his unconcern and lies, and then with myself, but I was terribly embarrassed too. *Why was I so trusting?* I sat in the waiting room and watched my husband leave, saying he had something to do. I couldn't believe he was leaving me. *What will I do now? Where is he going?* After what seemed like hours, a nurse came up to me and held my hand between hers. "We're ready to check you in now," she said.

"Are you sure you have the right person?"

"Yes, dear, I'm sure. You just need to concentrate on having a healthy baby."

Later that week, I learned my aunt had come to the hospital to see me and discovered what had happened. She withdrew money from her bank for the deposit.

Frank never told me what happened to the money, and I never asked. I guess I really didn't want to know what he did with it. I had better things on my mind.

At last, I would meet my baby. Seven hours after arriving at the hospital, my baby was born. Frank and I decided to call her Regina, which means "queen" in Spanish. Little Gina was the perfect baby. I was happier than I had been in years. While she was in the hospital nursery, people commented on the "baby that always smiled." She smiled all the time—when she was sleeping and when she was lying in my arms awake.

People said she looked like an angel; a special child. I knew she was special, because I never felt I could love anyone as much as I loved her. I talked to God a lot during that time. Not long after her birth, I prayed, "Father, Gina really belongs to You, not to me. Please guide this baby's life, and let her know how much You love her."

Once I held this sweet-smelling baby in my arms, I knew I would do anything for her.

"Gina," I said, fingering her thick, curly hair. "I'll make sure you are always safe. I love you so much, little one. You will have the very best life I can give you."

Gina was in perfect health, but since I had to have a caesarean section, I had to stay in the hospital a few more days. Although I was ready to begin my new family, I was grateful for the time to rest.

The day before I was to be discharged, Frank's aunt from North Carolina strolled into my hospital room carrying a box of brand-new baby clothes. I remembered how I was treated while in North Carolina after Frank's mother died.

"Hi," I said, wondering why she came. Just the sight of her turned my excitement to anger. Frank was standing beside me, and I wondered how he felt about what was happening.

"I've come to take the baby back to North Carolina," she said, "so you can get back to work." I watched her idly go through the baby clothes, all the while smiling and humming.

"My baby is not going anywhere!" I said. "Gina is staying with me. You can just leave the same way you came in."

Her smiling face suddenly turned hard. She grabbed up the baby clothes and stormed out the door. "We'll just see about that," she said.

Frank shot me a look that said, *If you were home, I'd make you sorry for this.* I returned a look that said, *Don't ever try to come between my child and me again. I will fight you with my last dying breath before I let you send her away.*

As long as I stayed in the hospital, I knew I was safe, but I couldn't stay forever. I remembered what Frank had said when I was pregnant—if he ever did anything; I was free to leave and take my baby.

For a moment, I felt the old fear settling in, but when my family arrived, I forgot about my anger and fear. I began to rejoice over my newborn daughter.

Finally, the day came for us to take Gina home. Frank arrived at the hospital, along with my mother, to have us discharged. He was a proud daddy. When the nurse handed Gina to him, a big smile erupted. I had never seen him so happy. *Maybe now he will really change and our lives and our marriage will turn out wonderful.*

CHAPTER X

The next day, I packed some clothes for Gina and me and went to my mom's house to stay for a while. That particular day, my Aunt Elizabeth happened to be visiting.

When we finished our small talk, I finally told them about the abuse. We talked for a long while. They saw how broken I was, and they cried with me.

"You need to go to court and get an Order of Protection," my mother finally said. My heart sank. How would that help? Frank would definitely kill me if he ever found out. I couldn't live in the court for my protection; I would have to find a place to live, and Frank knew so many people. What would stop him from finding me? It was a risk I was afraid to take.

However, I knew my time was running out. I had to do something, and it had to be soon. But now, though, my fear was so great, it almost crippled me.

Fear is a devastating spirit. It can make you feel as if you're losing your mind, and you begin to think of all the unpleasant things that can happen to you. At times, fear paralyzes you so much you're afraid to even move.

I had so much fear in me, I couldn't even think straight. Even a loud, unexpected noise made me jump. If I had just remembered, "For God hath not given us the spirit of fear; but of power, and of love, and of a sound mind" (2 Tim. 1:7, KJV), I would have handled it better.

An Order of Protection would be the first step to my independence. After mulling it over, I was still unsure of what would happen, but I knew I had to begin somewhere. All I needed was the courage. I knew what had to be done no matter how hard it was. I placed my trust in God, knowing He wouldn't leave me. I agreed to go to court.

Before I could put my plan into motion and get to court, Frank figured out where I was. When the phone rang that night, I answered. It was Frank.

"Why did you leave?" I couldn't believe he had the nerve to ask. He threatened me by saying I had better be back the next day, or he would come and get me, and I would be sorrier than ever.

"You know I could take Gina, and you would never see her again. You better not give me a hard time," he said.

Gina was safe where I was, for the moment, but if I wanted to live, I had to take some steps to protect us both. I made the decision to go to court, even though I was trembling with fear. Still, I knew I had to do it.

The next morning, along with my aunt, I went to Family Court. The court was full of other women experiencing some of the same things. Some were wearing casts because their husbands or boyfriends had beaten them. Others had bruises and sprains from having been thrown down a flight of stairs. I saw women with their heads wrapped in bandages, some walking on crutches, and some with neck braces. There were also those with no outward marks, but hurting inside. It was hard to fathom so many abused women. I realized with a start that it wasn't just happening to me!

> One thing I've learned and want to pass on to others in this situation: It is not your fault. What happened is nothing you have done or said; no one deserves to be beaten.

I never imagined seeing so many others like me in the courtroom. I thought I'd only be there a short while, but it was an all-day process. We began sharing our stories. It was eye-opening to realize how many women were going through similar situations. We talked as if we'd known each other for years.

While we waited, we sat in groups of three or four women. Although we would probably never see each other again, for those few hours, we found someone who understood. We had a common bond—we were being abused and desperately needed help; a way to escape.

Finally, the court clerk called my name, and as we did with each sister, the women said, "Good luck!" Encouraging words sounded throughout the courtroom. "Good for you." "You're taking a brave step." "You can do this!"

I had been interviewed by a caseworker earlier that morning, and the judge had my report in front of him when I was called. Although I had waited all day, the appearance before the judge took only a few minutes.

As the judge read my report, he began to shake his head. I had described some of my abuse to the caseworker, and the judge knew exactly what I had experienced. When he finished reading, he said he would most definitely grant me an Order of Protection, effective for three months. After that, if I wanted, I would have to repeat the same process again, but then the Order of Protection would be effective for a longer period of time. Finally, someone was on my side. It was a small victory, but a victory nonetheless.

Although I held the Order of Protection in my hands, I didn't feel protected. I knew Frank wouldn't feel threatened by a piece of paper. He would probably laugh; even destroy it. I was hesitant to follow through since in order for the Order of Protection to be effective, I had to give it to him. If we were in separate homes permanently, I reasoned, I could have someone else serve the papers.

I told the judge I was in temporary housing, but since I hadn't said "permanent housing" to him, in the court's eyes, I was still at home. To me, this Order of Protection could cause more trouble, putting me in danger—again! *How can I walk up to Frank and hand him this piece of paper?*

For a minute, I was tempted to toss it, but I knew without it, I had no proof of what was happening. My victory was short-lived when I came to the conclusion that even though I had the paper, my life was still in danger, maybe even more so.

As I walked out of the courtroom, I heard a commotion. A husband had located his wife, and came to the court to "change her mind." He had grabbed her and was about to hit her, when one of the court officers seized him and hauled him off to jail.

Her Order of Protection didn't do her much good. It really is just a piece of paper. I stayed here all day, and I'm still not safe! Maybe if Frank knew I had gone to court, and there was now a court record on him, he would think twice before putting his hands on me. Since he had no idea what an Order of Protection was, maybe it would scare him.

While I was away from my apartment, I stayed at my mother's house. To my relief, my mother or aunt stayed with Gina while I worked, and I tried not to worry. But it concerned me that she was missing time at the day-care center, and I knew eventually she would have to go back or begin somewhere else.

Gina needed to be a child. I knew if she could be with other children, it would take her mind off the problems at home. Maybe just playing with other children would keep her preoccupied. I knew I couldn't stay home with her. I had to continue to work in order to live and start a new life for us. I tried to act like everything was normal, and that we were just spending some time with Mama (her name for my mother).

For a while, Frank called me at least three times a day asking for forgiveness and swearing he would never hit me again. I knew he was lying and refused to show him any compassion. Finally, I stopped taking his telephone calls.

One night while Gina was spending the night at my aunt's, Frank called. He said he knew my every move, and that I was alone. He knew where I worked, where my mother worked, and what time she left for work. He knew my aunt's routine when she wasn't with Gina. I didn't want him to upset my aunt and, since she was elderly, I became frightened for her safety. What kind of a man would hit a woman and pick on an elderly woman?

You better come home! The words made me uneasy, but I stood my ground.

The threats continued almost every day. He threatened to take Gina from my aunt because she couldn't put up much of a fight. He said he didn't care about me, but he wanted his daughter, or else. In order to protect my family from any harm, I packed my things, and Gina and I returned home.

My mother couldn't believe I was going back. *You just don't understand. I'm doing it to protect you.*

I didn't even tell her about the threats until years later. I was afraid she would confront him and someone would get hurt. Knowing Frank, I knew he wouldn't be the one who got hurt. I knew his capabilities, and I couldn't allow my family to be harmed. He put a lot of thought into what he would do, and I believed him.

After I returned home, Frank was wonderful for a while, but I was used to his mood changes. Just as I thought, his sweet spirit was only temporary. The beatings became worse than before, and he made sure to remind me how he could hurt my family.

I lived in my own personal hell. Frank was out of control, and I had turned into someone I could no longer recognize. I didn't even like myself anymore. *How can I live like this? How can I put my child through this?* Nothing I did satisfied my husband.

If he felt the food wasn't good enough, he'd throw it on the floor and push me down to pick it up. When the telephone rang, he would answer it. If it was for me, before handing it to me he would say, "You've got five minutes." That meant if I stayed on any longer than five minutes, as soon as I got off, he would be ready to fight. He never even left the room, but stood right beside me listening to the conversation. I didn't want to provoke him, so I always said, "Oh, I smell something burning!" or, "I have to take care of Gina." I used any excuse I could to get off the phone on time. No one ever suspected that I was hanging up quickly for my own safety. In fact, people thought I didn't like to talk on the telephone much. My conversations were very short.

It's amazing that the rest of the world can't see when someone abuses another. It's a well-hidden secret. To the outside world, Frank was a perfect father and husband. Even my next-door neighbors never knew what was happening inside our apartment. Maybe if I had said something to them, Frank would have stopped or left. But he had convinced me that he would hurt anyone who knew. Besides, who would believe me? He could say I didn't know what I was talking about.

He didn't look like an abuser, but then, what does an abuser look like? I learned an abuser could look like anyone. They don't have any special characteristics.

One morning as I prepared breakfast, I heard an Inner Voice say, "I told you I would never leave you. You are special to me." At first, my heart skipped a beat, but then I felt completely at peace. I don't know how I knew, but I knew it was God speaking.

At almost the same moment, one of my neighbors knocked on the door. I let her in, and she came into the kitchen where I was pouring orange juice. "I just feel that I'm special to God," I said. "I can't explain it, but I just want you to know."

"Uh-huh. Right," she said. She gave me a "She's lost it!" smile and left. I felt a strange, new kind of strength and for the first time in years, I felt mentally strong. I thought about returning to church, but I had been away so long; I didn't even know where to begin. Besides, I was afraid I wouldn't be welcome.

In Brooklyn, New York, churches are everywhere, and I couldn't quite decide where to go. However, I learned that two of my neighbors were holding Bible studies in their homes, and I decided to join them. I wouldn't even have to leave the house; I could just walk across the hall. Even Frank was happy about that.

My friends said they would give the leaders of the study contact information about me. When the Bible study leaders came to my door, I invited them in. They seemed to be nice people who cared about me, and I began studying with them. But I had been raised a Christian, and I knew the Bible well enough to know that what they called the "Bible" was completely different from the one I remembered. I disagreed with some things, but they refused to change their views, saying that if I came to their place of worship, I would understand better.

I went one time, but knew I had to worship in a place that revered God's Word. I wanted to return to the church I knew and remembered. I wanted to sing the songs I was taught as a child. I wanted to feel the presence of God in the sanctuary, which I didn't feel at their church.

One cold, winter day, with snow flying from the skies, I said, "Frank, I want to go back to church—any church."

"God doesn't care about you," he said, laughing.

The Inner Voice I'd heard that day in the kitchen was as real as the snow piling up on the sidewalks. I held on tightly to what the voice said. *I am not crazy. God loves me. He will never leave me nor forsake me. I know that. How can I reach Him? He seems so far away.*

It seemed like the harder I tried to find God, the angrier Frank became. I remembered some of the songs I used to sing, and I even started reading my Bible. Although I didn't understand a lot of it, the words made me feel better; they gave me great comfort. However, Frank twisted my desire to seek the Lord into my looking for another man.

"Those men in the church only go there to find women, but you don't need to worry 'cause no man would ever look at you." I didn't care. I knew I had to keep searching for God regardless of what Frank said. *Please, Lord, I want to experience Your calmness in my spirit; Your peace that passes all understanding.*

CHAPTER XI

During my search for God, Gina began to sing songs she learned in day care, which reminded me of when I attended church with my mother, brother, and sister. God brought to mind the songs we used to sing, and Gina and I sang them together. This always seemed to send Frank into a rage. When we praise the Lord, we are aggravating the Evil One. He can't stand to hear our praise. He knows the power of praise, and it scares him because God blesses in the midst of praise.

One time while we were singing, Frank started hitting and pushing me, throwing things around, and breaking things, trying to distract Gina so she would stop singing, but she just kept singing louder. He never got angry with her, but the songs made him fight with me. Thank God she didn't stop, and I never tried to stop her. She seemed to know that any strength we needed came from the words of the songs she sang.

Whenever you believe you can't win, or the devil seems to be winning the battle, know that, ". . .the battle is not yours, but God's" (2 Chron. 20:15, NIV). And He has never lost a battle. Just hold on to your faith and keep trusting and believing in God. He will see you through.

That day, Gina continued to sing songs about the Lord, which made Frank want to fight. His rage became intense, and for a moment, I thought he would have a stroke. His fury caused the veins in his neck to bulge, and he said, "I'll get you for this."

Then he walked into another room, leaving us alone. Gina and I went to bed that night, and for the first time in a long time, I felt as though I was winning. My strength in God had never left.

The next morning I awoke in pain, and I found blood all over the sheets. For a moment I thought Frank had cut me while I was sleeping, but then I realized the blood was coming from inside of me. Frank had already left for work, and I began to panic.

I called my doctor, and he told me to go immediately to the hospital. I was hemorrhaging again. I had to call Frank to come home and take care of Gina. He was upset that I was inconveniencing him, but he came home anyway. Surprisingly, he drove me to the hospital, and then left, telling the staff that he had to take care of our child. They all thought how fortunate I was to have a husband who would do so much for me. They couldn't stop praising him enough. After all, he was the "perfect" husband. There weren't too many husbands who would be so caring.

Other people always seem to think abusers are the perfect husband or partner. The abuser makes sure no one, except the one being abused, sees them in their true light.

My friends in the medical profession at the hospital took good care of me. When I came out of the operating room, they bathed me, dressed me, and gave me a hot meal. They provided anything I wanted. I hadn't been pampered like that in years, and although it was a hospital, I would have been tempted to stay a little longer if I hadn't wanted to see Gina.

A few days later, Frank picked me up from the hospital and put on quite a show; holding my arm, telling me to be careful. He even said, "I can't wait to get you home" in such a way that the nurses sighed.

I felt the statement was not one of love; it was more of a threat. Once I arrived home, rest time and pampering were over. I couldn't take it easy because Frank was hungry, and I had to prepare his dinner. As usual, he felt if I was well enough to come home, I was healthy enough to cook.

Although I knew I was jeopardizing my health, I was determined that Gina would have something to eat. I didn't care if Frank ate or not, and no matter how crazy he acted, I truly believed he would never hit me while I was recuperating. I thank the Lord that He was taking care of me during this time and didn't allow anything to happen to me. The words He spoke to me forever sounded in my ears, "I will never leave you nor forsake you."

The next morning, I received a call from my doctor. He was concerned about my overall health. He said I was hemorrhaging too much, and if I weren't careful, he would have to do a hysterectomy. He was also troubled by my mental state. He felt I didn't care about myself anymore. He even thought I should seek the help of a psychiatrist. To him, I was a classic suicide candidate.

I had a hard time convincing him that no matter what I was going through, killing myself was not an option. In order to heal, he'd said, I was supposed to rest. Circumstances prevented it, and my visits to him were becoming too frequent.

"I just can't understand why you keep having these problems," he said. "Are you being abused? Is there something you want to talk about?" Of course, I never told him. I just did what I was supposed to and took care of Gina. She was the reason I was determined to live. I would never allow Frank's family to raise her. No matter what it took, I would survive and so would Gina. Though I was growing stronger in my faith every day, I had no idea my struggle was about to intensify.

Frank came home early one day. That's when I learned he'd lost his job. I took up the slack becoming the only one working again. He claimed he was looking for work, but our bills began piling up. I increased my hours to twelve hours a day, but most days I was so tired, I could barely put one foot in front of the other. If I ever complained, there would be a beating. So I kept quiet.

There was no way out. I was trapped in a world of abuse—physical and mental. The voice that said I was not alone seemed to be moving further away until finally, I felt maybe I had been crazy. *Did God really speak to me? Did He really say He would never leave me? Did I imagine the whole thing?*

Maybe Frank is right. I am in this alone. Every time I wanted to give up, though, a part of me would still fight. There was still a piece of me that said, "Hold on. Don't give up." I wanted that part of me to be quiet. *Why should I hold on? Why shouldn't I give up?* But the inner strength within me, the Holy Spirit, would not let me give up.

Every time I wanted to give up, I thought of Gina, and the struggle to survive returned. *Gina is my only reason for living. No one else cares what happens to me.* Frank had said it over and over: "Nobody cares what happens to you." I was beginning to believe it.

When you are brainwashed, you hear the same negative thing over and over, and even though it's not true, at some point, you begin to believe it.

I even began to think maybe I was the reason Frank turned into a monster. After all, he wasn't like that before we married, or I wouldn't have married him. In order to justify his abuse and my staying, I took all of the blame for his actions. Slowly, I sank deeper into depression.

CHAPTER XII

My mother and the rest of my family were beginning to worry about me. They rarely saw me, and when they did, I was too tired to be sociable. I didn't have much to say to anyone. I couldn't say much; I was afraid I would say the wrong thing. I made a point to go see them, so they wouldn't come to see me. I felt it necessary to bring Gina to see them or else they would become suspicious that my life wasn't going well.

Frank would drive me over for visits and then leave. By the time he came back, it was always late, and I'd have no time to rest before having to be at work for a late shift. He didn't care. Sometimes he never showed up, and Gina and I had to make it home the best way we could. Then I'd find Frank asleep on the couch claiming that time had slipped up on him.

On weekends, he usually stayed out, so Gina stayed with my family until I finished work. When she asked where her daddy was, I'd tell her he was working. That seemed to pacify her. I never said anything negative about him. She loved her daddy, and I didn't want to destroy that love. She could see what he was like each day and form her own opinion.

He never believed I didn't spend time talking about him, or trying to turn Gina against him. In his mind, all he believed I did was tell Gina how bad her father was. Whenever I talked to Gina in a low tone of voice, Frank drew near to hear what was being said. He didn't want me to speak to my child, and he always got angry when I wanted to spend time with my family. He didn't allow any of my friends to come to the house, either.

> Abusers isolate their victims from family and friends. In that way they can obtain complete control.

But my sister had a feeling something was wrong, and she started visiting me almost every Saturday. Finally, Gina and I had some company. My sister, Gina, and I listened to records, talked, and laughed for hours at a time.

My anxiety registered high most of the time my sister was at our apartment, because I was afraid Frank would walk in the door before my sister left. He hated when someone came by to visit me.

I tried not to think about it too much since Frank was rarely home on the weekends. And I welcomed my sister's visits, but couldn't quite rid myself of the fear that Frank might come home unexpectedly.

One day Gina, my sister, and I decided we wanted hamburgers from a certain restaurant, and we called a cab to drive us, wait for us, and bring us back. I knew I was spending extra money, but we had so much fun. We even joked about how the restaurants within walking distance—there was one right around the corner—weren't good enough.

I didn't think the few extra dollars I'd spent would matter. After all, Frank had found another job. I was wrong. When Frank came home, he was upset that I had spent the money, and threw the rest of the hamburgers and French fries into the garbage. I had no regrets, because I'd had such a wonderful time with my sister.

After my sister left, I felt the loneliness and fear creeping back in. But Gina was such a happy child. She always kept me smiling, and the loneliness would soon melt away into an afternoon of play. Sometimes, she just crawled into my lap and went to sleep, or she would bring her toys to me, and we'd play together. Soon, my sister, Gina, and I started going downtown for lunch on Saturdays. It was during these days out that I would take Gina to the photographer.

The trips continued after my nephew was born. My sister and I took our children for walks and shopping, and then visited the same photographer so the children could have photos made together. One day, we got tired of carrying them and bought identical strollers.

My nephew Jeffrey was like my own child. From time to time, I let him stay at my house while my sister babysat for Gina. She needed a break from her newborn son, and we traded. Surprisingly, Frank didn't have a problem with this. In fact, he thought it was a good idea. I always stepped lightly, never knowing what would make him angry, and I always took each day as it came.

Then Frank lost his job again, and I began working even longer hours, sometimes staying overnight at the hospital. There was a lot of possible overtime involved with my job, and I always volunteered for it. There was no other way—we needed the money. When I came home late at night, Gina often would be awake.

Whether it was late at night or early in the morning, she always waited for me to come home. If I left late at night, I would kiss her good night, and she'd go right to sleep. If I stayed at the hospital, I would call her. Frank let me talk to her, which was surprising. However, he stayed on the extension to listen to our conversation. I missed Gina and our time together, but if our bills were to be paid, if we were going to eat or have a place to live, I had to work.

I cooked extra meals during the week so Frank and Gina could have dinner, because Frank said cooking was woman's work. Evidently, so was heating up the food, because Frank wouldn't even do that. If he knew I was coming home, he wouldn't do anything. But, I must say he took good care of Gina. At one time, he said he wouldn't fix anything for her, but I knew he didn't mean it; his world revolved around his daughter. Plus, he knew that if I didn't work, no money would be coming in. I was exhausted and didn't know how much longer I could keep up the rigorous schedule. But I did, and I know it wasn't me or my strength, it was the strength of the Lord that helped me stand. I never could have done it on my own.

One day, I decided to go shopping for some new clothes without first telling Frank. When I came in with the packages, he was enraged. He grabbed the clothes from the bags and threw them around the room saying I was trying to look good, but that I was so ugly it didn't matter how many clothes I bought, they wouldn't help.

He cursed, and then pushed me toward the kitchen. While I stood there cooking, I again thought about killing Frank. As far as I was concerned, he had no right to live. About that time, Gina walked into the room and when I looked into her big, trusting eyes, I knew I couldn't do that to her. Frank was still her father.

One day as I headed toward the kitchen, I felt a sharp pain in my stomach, which caused me to double over. I screamed. Frank ran into the kitchen, took one look at me and made me sit down. He finished getting supper ready. *Amazing!* Once again, he was a caring husband. The pain was so excruciating, I felt I as though I would vomit or pass out. Frank helped me to the bed, but it was too painful to lie down. There was so much tenderness inside of me I could hardly tolerate the bed linens touching my stomach.

The pain became so intense I felt I couldn't stand any more of it. But suddenly, the pain disappeared as soon as it had come. Then Frank said I was just trying to get attention. *So much for the caring husband.*

Gina raced into the bedroom to see why I had screamed and, in spite of the pain; I smiled to assure her that everything was fine. Frank said he would take care of me, but the look he shot my way said he didn't mean it. I turned to go into the kitchen, and the pain ripped through me again. I ran into the bathroom feeling if I could just vomit, I'd feel better.

"The theatrics won't work! You can pretend all you like, but I'm not buying it," Frank said. The room was spinning, and I again felt as if I would faint. For a moment, I felt if I could die, I wouldn't have to suffer anymore, but when I thought of Gina growing up without me, I received new strength. I straightened up and walked back into the bedroom to lie down for a while. Frank had promised to finish dinner, but I knew about his empty promises. Still, I had no choice but to trust him. I couldn't make it into the kitchen.

Just as I was about to lie down, I heard Gina screaming. I ran into her bedroom and found her almost hysterical.

I grabbed her up in my arms and she continued to scream. "Mommy, there's a man behind you. He's going to hurt you!" I turned around and didn't see anything, but I felt a presence.

"I don't see anyone, Gina," I said, but she insisted he was going to hurt me. I wish I'd been more spiritually strong. If I had been, I would have prayed God's protection over us. As it was, I could only hold her and tell her no one would hurt us.

Even with all the commotion and screaming, Frank never came to see what was wrong. I felt there was an evil presence manifesting in the apartment. Gina saw whatever it was even at her young age. It was so real, I thought if I turned around someone would be standing there even though I knew there was no one else in the apartment. *What was wrong with me? Was I imagining things?*

Then, a strange odor wafted through the room. It made me gag and gasp for air. While I calmed Gina, the odor vanished. She begged me not to leave, and as soon as we felt calmed, we lay down on her bed and dozed. By now the pain had left, and Frank finished cooking our meal.

I was worried about the pain I had experienced, but I was even more concerned because my period was late. Later that week when I went to the doctor, she said I might be pregnant. I always wanted lots of children and had prayed for a large family, but now was not the time. I thank the Lord that He gives us what we need, not what we want. He promises to supply all our needs. "And my God will meet all your needs according to his glorious riches in Christ Jesus" (Phil.4:19, NIV).

Although I had always wanted a houseful of children, I definitely didn't need any more right now. However, God has answered my prayer for many children in His own way, because I do have a lot of children. They are the ones that God has led me to nurture—Gina's friends who call me "Mom," and those who I refer to as my "spiritual" children.

Three days later, it was confirmed. I was pregnant. When Frank came home, I told him, and he began to yell. "How could you be so stupid? We can't have another child!" When I told him it takes two people to make a baby, his answer was a punch to my face.

Wiping blood from my mouth, I went to my room and cradled my belly. I told this unborn child that no matter what, I would always make sure he or she felt loved.

The following month, though, I began to hemorrhage. There would be no baby. Frank just shrugged his shoulders. He didn't allow me to mourn because he said I was being stupid. He said, "It wasn't really a baby." It was one more thing I buried deep inside. I was learning to hide my feelings very well.

A few days later, the bleeding continued, and it wouldn't stop. I became very weak and called the doctor. She told me to get to the hospital and made arrangements for me to have another procedure. It was the same routine. I stayed overnight, had someone check me out and returned home only to be abused again. I was supposed to stay off my feet, but I was back at work the next day. The rent was due.

Soon afterwards, I began working at another hospital. I always had to change jobs because my coworkers became suspicious. I knew it meant even longer hours, but we needed the money. In the beginning, the job worked out fine and the money helped.

One day, while riding the subway to work I began to sweat profusely. The familiar pain in my abdomen returned with a vengeance. The train roared into Manhattan, and someone offered me a seat, but I hurt so badly, I couldn't move. When we arrived at my destination, I stumbled out the door, barely able to shuffle one foot in front of the other. I *willed* myself to get to work. When I arrived, the pain was so bad I could barely speak. All I could do was focus on the pain. The pain was so intense, my legs buckled whenever I tried to stand.

Just like my previous experience when the pain felt as though it would make me pass out, it again mysteriously stopped. I continued working and at lunchtime, I felt sick again. I could no longer stand up to perform my job, and I had no choice except to go home. Only this time, someone called a taxi for me. I couldn't take the chance of riding the subway again.

When Frank came home, I explained what happened, and he seemed somewhat concerned. For the first time in a long time, he offered to take care of Gina so I could rest. He even went out and bought a meal for us. The pain had eased, and I was able to eat. Later the pain stopped, so I didn't call the doctor. *What is wrong with me? The pain is on-again, off-again. Will this not-so-merry-go-round ever stop?*

I knew I had to continue to work and take care of my child. Besides, the pain had been there before, and it always stopped. I wasn't too concerned, and I surely didn't want to go into the hospital again. For one thing, the medical staff was beginning to recognize me. They were calling me by my first name and making comments like, "What are you doing here again, Bonita?" Those comments told me it was time to move on.

One day, Frank came home with a pocketful of money. He said he'd found *another* job, and they paid him in advance. In fact, he and Gina had taken a taxi home. I had come home early because of the mysterious pain. I asked him where he worked, because I had never heard of a job where they provided such a large amount of money on the first day. He began to scream at me and balled up his fist.

I suddenly snapped, and I began to lash out in spite of how bad I felt. This time, I would be the one to inflict pain; to leave bruises. I wanted him dead or at least in intense pain! Nothing else mattered. I kicked, I scratched, and I bit, but he didn't seem to feel any of it. He began to laugh and went in the living room to watch television as though nothing had happened. *He is not human! How can he not feel anything?* I had hit, kicked, and bit him with all my might. When I walked into the living room, he looked at me in disgust and returned to watching television. He gave me a look that said, "Stupid. What were you thinking?"

My explosive anger seemed to have removed the pain momentarily, and I started dinner.

Gina was in her bedroom doing her homework, and with her door closed, she couldn't hear anything. I opened the door, and she gave me the biggest smile I had ever seen. She ran to give me a quick "Mommy, I love you" hug, and then returned to her homework. She loved school, and we never had to pressure her to do her homework. In fact, she looked for things to write and bring to me. I thank God for Gina because no matter how bad things became, I could always look at her and think of a thousand reasons for living. I thanked God she didn't have the disposition of her father.

The stress of trying to deal with my husband's moods began to wring every ounce of energy from me. My stomach pains returned, but every time I visited the doctor, she couldn't find anything out of the ordinary. I had a high stress job, and the doctors thought it might be an ulcer. They wanted to do tests, but Frank wouldn't hear of it. His *job* kept him busy, and he couldn't take extra time to watch Gina so I could have the tests done. My mother worked, and my aunt, who occasionally took care of Gina, was getting older. I didn't want to tire her. I finally resigned myself to the fact that maybe they were right; maybe it was the stress. After all, the pain was like a yo-yo; it would always go away as quickly as it came.

Sometimes the pain woke me up, but it seemed to move to other spots and give me some relief. I had to work, so I pushed myself a little harder knowing I had no choice except to keep moving. One morning the pain was so bad, I didn't think I could even crawl out of bed.

I wanted to stay home, but I had to take Gina to school because Frank left for work early. After dropping Gina at school, I headed for the subway. When I neared the subway, I felt the pain sear my stomach, but I forced myself to keep going.

At work, the pain increased and seemed to gravitate toward my back. By lunchtime, I thought eating might help, so I ate a small lunch. I felt some relief, but an hour later, I doubled over in immense pain. I told my boss I was sick, but he said it wasn't a good time to take off. Instead, he told me to go to Health Services, but the pain subsided, and I didn't seek any medical attention. I finished working that day.

One night as Frank, Gina, and I watched the movie, "Roots," I felt it would be a peaceful evening together with my family. We were all in one room and there hadn't been even the first cross word between Frank and me.

We decided to let Gina watch some of the program, because it was time for her to learn about her heritage. Frank had been quiet all evening, and we were all relaxed. Just when I felt more content than I had been in a long time, the pain struck with a vengeance.

Because of its intensity, I had a feeling this time the pain wouldn't go away.

"Frank, please call an ambulance."

But Frank looked at me as if I'd lost my mind. He continued to watch the program. I struggled to the telephone and called my mother; this was no time to argue with my husband.

"Mom," I said, gasping for breath, "this pain is the worst it's ever been. Can you come get me?" She didn't even hesitate, but came right away. Frank stayed with Gina, and my mother let him know how disappointed she was that he wouldn't bother to take me to the hospital.

When I arrived at the hospital, I was admitted right away. I had fainted in the taxi on the way over. My blood pressure was elevated, and I was in so much pain they had to medicate me immediately. My mother said I kept slipping in and out of consciousness.

The doctors had no idea what was wrong, but decided to admit me. When I finally got a room, the doctors continued to check on me all night. The pain was so brutal, I couldn't bear for any of them to touch me. The doctors said it was a mystery. They couldn't find a reason for my pain.

The next morning, I was scheduled for more tests. After awhile, I was told I needed major surgery; my gall bladder was full of stones. They said I was lucky to be alive, because the accumulated gallstones could have poisoned my system.

God was still taking care of me even though I didn't think He cared anymore. I didn't understand. I hadn't been to church in awhile. *Why would He care about me? I had forsaken going to church. I had even put my family before Him.*

I heard God's words again. They seemed to ring in my ears. *I will never leave you nor forsake you.*

Frank never came to the hospital, and he had no idea how serious my illness was. The pain finally subsided because of the medication. From my hospital bed, I asked to see Gina, but my mother had already talked to her and assured her I would be fine.

My mother also said Frank made several excuses about not going to the hospital. I knew it was because he was afraid he had done something to cause what happened to me. I really didn't care if he came or not and prayed he would be packed and gone by the time I returned home. *Why is he staying? There's no marriage left.*

The attendants wheeled me down to surgery, and I whispered, "If anything happens to me, Lord, please take care of Gina. Don't let her fall into the wrong hands. Keep Your hand on her, Lord." Maybe this was how my life would end. I felt a comforting peace settle over me after I prayed. Gina would be fine. She was God's child. I remembered telling Him that if I had a child, I would raise her for Him, and I knew He remembered.

In the operating room, I was relaxed, and it wasn't from the medication. It was the kind of peace that said things would work out. It was the "peace that passes all understanding" that could only come from God.

The anesthesiologist placed the mask over my face, and I drifted off. In what seemed like a matter of minutes, I heard someone on the telephone saying, "We need you to come to the hospital right away. There were complications." The next thing I heard was "The patient is alive, cancel the call." The amazing thing about this is, there are no telephones in the operating room. *Lord, are You trying to tell me something?* Yet, I know what I heard. I was taken into recovery, and the next time I opened my eyes I was in my room.

"I have never seen so many gallstones," the doctor said, "but the operation went well without any complications." He noted something on my chart, and then added, "You are one lucky woman, your gallbladder could have burst with that many stones. It's a miracle your system wasn't completely poisoned."

The day I was to be discharged from the hospital, I hoped Frank wouldn't show up. Gina was staying with my mother, so I knew she was well cared for. When I saw Frank walking up the hall, I was disappointed. I remember thinking, *Why couldn't he have gotten in an accident?* He acted like a concerned, loyal husband. The nurses were impressed with his concern for me. One of them even commented how lucky I was to have someone who cared so much about me. She said, "Girl…you better hold onto him. Someone could snatch him!"

CHAPTER XIII

For the next few months, Frank was every woman's dream. He came home every day, took care of Gina, and took her to school and brought her home. He even tried to prepare some meals and was always in a good mood. When he burnt a meal, or it tasted terrible, we laughed. I foolishly thought that maybe he had changed for good.

I found myself letting my guard down. Maybe my illness had scared him silly, and he was trying to make up for how he'd treated me in the past. Maybe he had no choice but to take care of me. After all, my family was constantly visiting me, and he had to keep up the pretense of being a good husband. However, it didn't last long. As soon as I was cleared to go back to work, Frank went back to being his old self.

"Frank, the rent is late." I sprayed the coffee table with furniture polish and began to dust.

"I'm sorry," he said, menacingly. "I forgot. It's your fault for not reminding me!"

I heard footsteps behind me, and I turned. Before I could say anything, he pushed me with such force that I bounced against the wall and slid down.

In his anger, he shouted, "I can't come home from working hard and do everything in the house too!"

He came home with plenty of money, yet the rent was still late. *Why couldn't he pay it? What was going on?* It was happening again. Again, I fought to keep my sanity.

I'd changed jobs and had begun to work for the doctor who had performed my surgery. It was only a few minutes away from the apartment, and I could take a bus or taxi to work. I still worked overtime, but it meant that I could get home quicker.

I began having nightmares. I would awake with a start, believing someone was in the room with me. The feeling was so real; I could almost hear someone breathing. But when I woke up, nothing was there. Getting up in the morning became harder and harder. My friendly neighbors had moved, and there was no one to talk to anymore. Frank still wouldn't let me have any friends. He said friends would only try to get into our business.

I felt trapped. In my mind, there was no way out. The only thing I wanted was for my five-year-old daughter to be happy, and I couldn't provide that by myself. Gina adored her father and despite how much he hated me, he worshipped her. How could a man have so much love in him for one person and have just as much hate for another?

Then one day, we were told to move. The landlord said, "You need to move because my children are growing up, and I want more space."

I knew, though, it was because of our noisy fighting. In a way, I felt relieved. *Maybe now we can start over. I will do anything to make our marriage work.*

Frank wanted a certain upscale type of apartment. He had expensive tastes, but he didn't want to use his money from his mysterious *job*. Finally, we found an apartment in the Flatbush section of Brooklyn, and I was more than happy to leave those unpleasant memories behind.

Our new, large apartment building had a doorman and was in a very good neighborhood with plenty of nice stores. I knew it would take longer to get Gina to school, but it was okay. I finally had a large kitchen connected to an equally large dining area. It was the kind of apartment I always wanted. Before I went to sleep one night, I prayed everything would change; that we would become a real, loving family. Then, the unbelievable happened.

A woman's screams pierced the night. It sounded as though it came from the hallway. Frank and I jumped up, checked on Gina, and then ran to the door. Our next-door neighbor held a baseball bat above his head while chasing his wife through the hall. Frank just shrugged his shoulders.

Please let him see himself in that man. May he understand what he's been doing to me.

I reached for the phone to call the police. Frank grabbed the telephone from me. "If you pick that up again, I'll break it over your head. Do you understand?"

Things hadn't changed a bit. I went back to bed, but I couldn't keep the woman's screams from pulsing in my head.

The next day, I watched the couple leave for work with their arms around each other. Of all the places in the city to live, we lived next door to a couple that fought every day. It seemed cruel that I lived next door to the nightmare I was trying to escape.

What else can go wrong?

The answer was, Frank could get worse. Not only did I have violence in my home, it was also right next door.

I planned to make the best of my bad situation. I found a bakery around the corner and decided to surprise Frank by buying sweet rolls for his breakfast. I felt maybe he would be in a better mood if he satisfied his sweet tooth.

Unfortunately, he seemed angry every day now. That Saturday morning, I heated the sweet rolls. I knew he would be surprised at my thoughtfulness, and maybe he would be happy for a change. I boiled the water for coffee and put his favorite breakfast on the table.

I had gotten up early to prepare a special breakfast just for my husband and was anxious to see how he would react. Frank sat down.

"Here, Gina, have a roll," I said, handing her a plump one.

Frank frowned, but I ignored it. Maybe he was tired. After all, he had been out all night with his friends. After the water boiled, I poured some into my cup.

Without warning, Frank jumped up, grabbed the cup and threw the boiling water in my face. My face felt like it was on fire, and when I leapt up, he came up behind me and punched my ear. *I feel so dizzy. . .I can barely focus.*

"You gave away the roll I wanted!" he screamed. *Amazing!* He was mad because he couldn't have the roll he wanted.

"Leave my mother alone!" cried Gina. It was the first time she'd ever said anything. Frank's eyes filled with rage. He had never hit her or even spanked her, but I could see it wouldn't take much to push him over the edge. And I wasn't going to let that happen. I wouldn't stand for that.

"You better tell her to go to her room," he said under his breath.

"It's all right, Gina. You can go into your room and play. You can even take some food with you to feed your dolls."

This was new. Frank was now abusing me in front of Gina. He didn't seem to care if she knew. I was so angry at what he'd done that I kicked him. He was still stronger than I was, and he overpowered me, throwing me to the floor.

After we'd moved in our new apartment, we had planned to replace the carpet we had pulled up, but we hadn't done it yet. The nails that still stuck through the wood caught my hands and legs, ripping them. Blood ran down my legs and hands. I picked up a dining room chair and threw it at him.

He laughed, slamming the door as he walked out. As soon she heard the door slam, Gina came out and threw her arms around me.

"Mommy, I love you so much. Don't you worry; I will always take care of you."

She went into the bathroom and brought me a wet washcloth to wash the blood off. Then she said, almost whispering, "Now, can we finish eating?"

I laughed out loud. Leave it to a child to de-stress a situation. Gina and I ate as though nothing had happened, then she went to her room to play with her toys. She seemed satisfied that everything was all right.

I sat in the living room alone, and did something I hadn't done in a long time.

I bowed my head and asked, "God, what can I do?" Although I had stopped attending church, I remembered my Uncle Ernest saying, "You can talk to God any time."

I also remembered that small, still voice that said, "I will never leave you nor forsake you."

The Devil likes to put thoughts in our minds that we believe are our own. I never learned about lining things up with the Word of God. If I had studied the Word, I would have known about "bringing every thought into captivity to the obedience of Christ " (2 Cor.10:5b, NKJV).

God, why am I going through all of this turmoil? Is it because of something I've done?

I felt defeated and alone. Broken dishes and pieces of food littered the floor.

What a mess this place is—just like I am.

Though I'd cried many times, I couldn't stop the tears flowing down my face. I sobbed until I could hardly breathe. My head ached.

When I finally stopped crying, I noticed the apartment seemed to be full of an unnerving presence—in my mind, something evil. I felt as if it were watching my every move. Every time I turned around, I just knew someone stood nearby. It was as though a dark cloud hung over everything in the apartment. Gina felt it too. She left her room and to feel secure, she followed me everywhere. Finally, I told her we would go for a walk.

Our apartment was near Prospect Park, and we walked to the park, over to McDonald's, and returned home. We giggled and talked all of the way. Soon, I dismissed the idea of an evil presence inside our apartment.

When I turned the corner, our apartment building loomed in front of us, and my mood quickly changed. Gina and I started walking slower, postponing the inevitable. When the elevator doors closed in front of me, I felt as if the doors to my freedom had closed too.

The minute I opened the door to my apartment, I felt the unnerving presence again. I dismissed it as my imagination and fixed supper.

"Mommy, will you stay in my room? Just until I get to sleep?"

"Sure, baby, I'll be here." I hummed a familiar song until her eyelids drooped, and she dropped off to sleep.

When Frank came in late, he smelled of perfume.

"It's just samples from one of my friends," he said. "She sells beauty supplies and sent you some things." He put a bag full of lotions, perfume, and bath oil on the dresser.

"Thank you," I said in a tone of voice that sounded like I didn't mean it, and walked away.

"You're just ungrateful!" he shouted, throwing the bag across the room. Its contents spilled across the floor. *How else should I act when my husband comes home smelling of women's perfume? Am I supposed to be happy his "friend" sent me beauty supplies?*

I put on a gown and headed toward the bed. Out of my peripheral vision, I thought I saw someone standing in the room. I blinked, but it was gone.

Momentarily, a chill coursed down my spine. I ignored the feeling, and went to bed. Later that night, I heard Gina scream.

I raced into her room.

"Someone is in the room, Mommy!" Her small body quivered as she clung to me.

"Nobody's here, Gina," I said as calmly as I could. "See?" I turned on the light, and I checked in her closet, behind the door, and under her bed.

Intellectually, I knew it was impossible for anyone to be in the room, but my instincts said otherwise. I recalled Gina had seen something in the other apartment too.

Was something following us?

I put my hand on her head, leaned down and kissed her forehead. "Gina, God's not going to let anything happen to you. Now try to go back to sleep."

"Mommy, it's not going to hurt me; it wants to hurt you." She tugged on my nightclothes, trying to keep me from leaving.

"If you stay with me, Mommy, nothing will happen to you."

"Baby girl, I'm fine." I sat down on the bed until Gina relaxed and went back to sleep.

"Lord, please take care of my child," I whispered.

An evil thought penetrated my mind. *God doesn't care what you ask for. He doesn't even know you.*

I put down the evil thought. I knew God would take care of my little girl. On my way back to bed, I thought I heard laughter. It seemed to be surfacing from every wall in the apartment.

Am I losing it? Am I finally going crazy? I stopped my thought process before it could go further. *You can't go crazy; you have to raise Gina.*

I went into the bedroom where Frank was murmuring in his sleep. He put his hands up, and then grimaced in pain. The next minute he was laughing. I found a blanket and went to the living room to sleep. I didn't know what his problem was, but whatever it was, he'd have to deal with it on his own.

The next morning, I woke up feeling as if I'd been beaten. I found bruises on my arms and legs. Again, I dismissed it. Deep down, I knew something was happening that was beyond my comprehension, but I knew I wasn't going crazy.

For the first time in a long time, I wanted to attend church. When I told Frank, he said I better not go—or else! I knew what that statement meant, so I decided not to go. Instead, I prepared breakfast. As I fixed the food, thoughts ran through my mind: *How could I walk into a church and act like I knew God? Sure, I had prayed earlier for protection, but I didn't really know Him.*

My life was miserable, and I didn't want anyone in church to ask me what was wrong. In my defense, I did go to church a few times when Gina was a baby, but I drifted away. Gina loved church from the time she was little. She always slept peacefully until the service was over. I enjoyed it too, but the fights afterward prevented me from going.

Frank's constant theme was, "You only want to go to church to find a man." He always felt church was for socializing, not learning about God.

"Anybody can read a Bible and scream a few times, then take people's money," he said.

Gina attended a Christian school where she learned a lot of songs and read the Bible every day. At home, she began to recite different scriptures. Then, she showed me the things she'd learned in the Bible, and she'd sing praise songs she learned in school.

One day, she came home and excitedly said, "Mommy, I'm going to sing with my class at the church. Will you come? Please?"

"Of course I will, Gina." I'd always supported her in everything she did. Frank, of course, said he would be too busy.

That Sunday, as we prepared to leave, I felt a kind of excitement I couldn't explain. I could hardly wait to get there. We arrived early, and when I walked into the sanctuary, I remembered going to church as a little girl with my brother and sister. We always sat in the second row behind the stewardesses or "the ladies in the white dresses" as we called them.

My mother was the musician and everyone knew us. I reminisced about my days in Sunday school, and how much I enjoyed walking to church every Sunday morning with the other children. I recalled the plays, recitals, and services in which I played a part. I had been raised in the church and went two or three times a week. I thought of the times I prayed and sang to God, and I knew He was listening.

What happened to me? Where did I make a wrong turn? I loved church so much I would cry when I couldn't go. What went wrong?

I liked the people at Gina's school and became friends with one of the children's parents. Although she always talked about her church, she was critical about other places of worship. She felt that other denominations were doctrinally wrong in many areas, including baptism and marriage.

She talked about other parents, making snap judgments and saying things like they weren't saved. One thing that bothered me most was that she said she couldn't understand why people wanted to honor Martin Luther King Jr. "He wasn't that great," she said, "In fact, if he had minded his business, he would be alive today."

I knew her church was not the right one for me. One thing I always remembered was that God is love, and there was no love in this woman's discussion about her church.

One day, I made plans to return to church and go every Sunday, no matter what Frank said. As the day drew nearer, I knew I would have to tell him. When I told him my plans, he said I couldn't go. Something rose up in me, and I said in no uncertain terms, "I am going! I don't care what you say, I *will* go to church."

That day, he backed off.

I was excited about going back to church. I told Gina we were going, and I could see the light in her eyes shine. She talked about it all week and when Sunday morning came, she was the first one up and the first one dressed. She twirled around the apartment, excitement filling her face. I knew people at this church, and we enjoyed the services.

It felt good to be back in a loving and caring church, and I began to feel that, although I had been through a lot, I would be all right. I felt the warmth and love of other saints that I hadn't felt in a long time.

God's protection surrounded me as long as I was in the church. Sometimes, though, the thoughts of my abuse would creep back in, but the thoughts would leave quickly. I felt as if a heavy burden had been lifted from my shoulders. If I could live inside the church, I would. Nothing and no one could harm me inside God's refuge—"God is our refuge and strength, an ever-present help in trouble" (Psalm 46:1, NIV). For the first time in a long time, I felt as though I belonged. I smiled all the time, and no one had cause to ask if I was all right. My countenance showed it; I laughed and sang and prayed. I rejoiced when I sang the older songs I used to sing. A new strength took over my body—the strength of the Lord!

As we left the church, I felt a strange feeling, almost as if something bad was about to happen. It was as if a cool wind blew across my body, and the chill lingered awhile, taking away the love and warmth I had experienced inside the church. I ignored it and, after buying Gina a snack, we headed home. Gina was excited, and she talked and giggled all the way home. Even people on the bus were smiling because her childish joy was infectious.

"Oh, Mommy," she said, "I can't wait to go back. I had so much fun!" She threw back her head and laughed so hard that I joined her. By the time we got back to the building, my sides ached.

As soon as I walked in, Frank's eyes narrowed, and he shot me that familiar look.

"How long does it take for church to end? Are you meeting someone? If you are, I guarantee I'll find out about it, then you know what will happen!" He squared his jaw, and then added, "I'll kill you both."

"Frank, I need to go to church. I need the Lord . . ."

"Yeah," he said, "you're probably having an affair. Is it the pastor?"

"Give me a break, Frank." I sat down on the sofa and stared at my living room wall. Then with a power I didn't know existed inside me, I added, "I *will* go to church every Sunday!"

Right before my eyes, his face seemed to contort. In my growing fear, I didn't even remember all I had to do was call upon the name of the Lord, and I would have been safe. The fear paralyzed me. Frank looked different; like someone I didn't know. His eyes blazed like white-hot copper.

My fear melted into peace. I couldn't explain it, but the peace made me smile.

How can I smile when this vile man is standing in front of me and threatening me?

Frank went into the bedroom like nothing had happened, and I began to start our dinner. God's Word is true, "For the battle is not yours; but God's" (2 Chron. 20:15b, NIV). I had spent time that morning with the Lord and His power was still on me.

Gina walked into the kitchen, sat at the table and began to sing some songs she had heard at church. I joined in. "From the lips of children and infants you have ordained praise" (Psalm 8:2, NIV).

The two of us were having a good time, and the previous events were soon forgotten. In fact, there was a peace in the house I hadn't felt for a while. And the presence had not reappeared. Finally, I was able to smile again and keep smiling. Frank didn't leave the room. He didn't dare—God's power was in the house.

That week at work, some of my coworkers commented that I looked different, more at ease, and I told them I'd been to church. I felt a new strength, a power, and I knew it was because I'd been with God.

The hunger for God multiplied, and I was excited about returning to church the next Sunday. I wanted to be there to worship as much as possible.

I decided to buy new clothes for Gina and me, because I didn't want us to look out of place. I know, of course, that "man looks at the outward appearance, but the Lord looks at the heart" (1 Sam. 16:7b, NKJV). I still had a human desire to fit in, so I went shopping.

That day, Frank laughed. "It doesn't matter what you buy, it won't help."

I ignored him and went shopping anyway. Gina's face shone with pure joy as I purchased her new church clothes. She couldn't wait to wear them.

Whenever I talked about church, Frank became enraged. He almost seemed afraid of my going to church. During the week, he talked about the pastor and made up all sorts of stories. By Sunday, he would try any trick he could to get me to stay home.

I attended church, and when I returned home, Frank would be waiting to start a fight. He said if I stopped going to church, he would stop hitting me. I knew if I stopped going, I would be in worse danger— danger of losing my soul (Matt. 10:28, NIV).

Soon, I began feeling at home in the church, and a few months later I joined, was baptized, and became a member. I was talking to God more and more, and my life seemed wonderful.

It was hard enough trying to get into a habit of praying unceasingly to God, but hearing His small, still voice was even harder.

CHAPTER XIV

The Holy Spirit tried to warn me about Rhonda, but I shut His voice out. I ignored Him when I met Rhonda—one of the friendliest people I'd met in a long time.

Rhonda had a nice voice, and she and her two daughters sang in the choir. Sometimes when Rhonda praised God, she could not even finish the song before she ended up dancing and shouting throughout the church.

How wonderful Rhonda feels so blessed that she is comfortable praising the Lord through dancing and shouting. I certainly can't do it. The Holy Spirit's insistent warning just has to be wrong. She loves the Lord.

Although she didn't know everything about Frank and me, she knew something wasn't right. Many times, she invited me to her home just to sit and talk.

In hindsight, I should have questioned the candles placed around Rhonda's living room. Or the African statues she kept in her bedroom. I was naïve, I guess, but I didn't know those were considered idols, and not things of God. Some of the statues had interesting, even distorted, faces but to me they were just art. Although I didn't feel comfortable about these objects, I shrugged the warnings off.

How can I feel uncomfortable about a piece of art?

Besides, Rhonda was always in church; always praising and praying. I foolishly thought that it was just another level to her faith when she began to talk about the African gods connected to these statues.

Back then, I had no idea how important it was to know the Word of God and to come into a relationship with Him. I couldn't just know of Him, I needed to *know* Him. Satan enters as an angel of light. He is a liar and can deceive us into thinking he is of God when, in fact, he is trying to pull us into his kingdom.

One day, I sat in Rhonda's living room, sharing my trials. "I feel like I am going crazy, Rhonda. It's harder and harder to hold on."

"I understand," she said, nodding. "I want you to meet someone. She'll be able to help you."

That someone wanted to pray for me, so I went with her into a prayer room where she had a table with statues of "Jesus" and candles.

"This is where I feel the presence of God," the woman said. As she prayed, I began to feel nauseated. The room began to dim, and with every passing second, it grew darker. Then I vomited.

"You're being cleansed," she said. I accepted her explanation, because I didn't know any better.

I can understand how people get caught up in these idolatrous rituals. In my case, I had been feeling left out. I felt as though I wasn't growing in the Lord as quickly as I should. I had been abused for so long that I longed for any small kindness. In some ways I was brokenhearted; brokenhearted over the loss of my life. That's when corrupt people begin to take advantage—when they see your weakness. But I know the Lord cares for the brokenhearted. I know that, "He healeth the broken in heart, and bindeth up their wounds" (Psalm 147:3, KJV).

I felt alone, and I began to finally trust someone—Rhonda. Since I could talk so freely to her, I never dreamed she would involve me in anything ungodly. When I left the "prayer room," I felt as if a giant plank were laid on my shoulders.

When I mentioned this terrible burden to Rhonda, she blamed Frank. Sadness engulfed me, and I wanted to cry. She told me the Lord couldn't get through to me because of what Frank was doing.

"There is a church I'd like you to visit," she said. "Then you'll understand the moving of the spirit."

That Sunday evening, I walked into the church and immediately felt uncomfortable. The lights were so dim; I could hardly make out the pews, the people, or anything else.

I sat down next to Rhonda and listened to the singing. While it was all right, some of the church members seemed unfriendly.

I didn't know the Word really well, but I did know I serve a loving God. Some of those people didn't seem to have love in them.

Sitting in that service, I promised I would never return. I couldn't put my finger on it, but I knew these people were not who they claimed to be. "Not every one that saith unto me, 'Lord, Lord' shall enter into the kingdom of heaven" (Matt. 7:21a, KJV). We need to see what kind of fruit comes from people and what kind of life they are living. Do they preach Jesus Christ and Him crucified? That's what we look for. I thank God for His teachings.

I began to panic. *Lord, just get me out of here. I know this is not of You.*

Once I left the building, I realized the Holy Spirit was warning me. I thank God for the Holy Spirit!

God's Word says, "My people are destroyed from lack of knowledge" (Hosea 4:6, NIV). How true! I could have been destroyed because of my lack of knowledge. But God loves His children, and I thank Him that He didn't give up on me and protected me by reminding me of scripture and revealing that I would know them by their fruit.

After realizing I'd stepped away from God, and almost become ensnared in Satan's trap, my heart felt heavy with grief.

Father, I am so sorry I sinned. Forgive me, Lord, for walking down a wrong path—the wide path that leads to destruction. I am Your child and right now, I declare the Devil has no right to me. Thank You for loving me and for standing by my side.

CHAPTER XV

It was a 95-degree, sweltering-hot summer, and I was glad that Gina had the opportunity to visit Frank's family in North Carolina. I couldn't make it, because I didn't have enough vacation time.

Frank surprised me when he said he was going to North Carolina for a week and taking Gina with him. But worry never entered my mind. He was a loving father and had never harmed her. He truly loved his daughter. Besides, it was only a week, and she would be with family. They loved her and always treated her good, going out of their way to show her a great time. I packed enough clothes for a week and kissed Gina good-bye.

While they were away, I spent quality time with my mother. When I called to check on Gina, she was so busy playing, I asked them not to disturb her.

As the week progressed, I never questioned that I had only spoken to her once, because every time I called she was either playing or visiting another family member. I missed her terribly, but I knew she needed to spend time with the other side of the family.

The week seemed to drag and finally, on the day they were supposed to return, I came home early and prepared a large meal. When Frank walked in the door, I thought Gina was hiding. I ran into the hall to greet her, but she wasn't there.

Frank shrugged his shoulders, "She didn't feel like coming back," he said, "so I left her."

My world stopped turning. *Did I understand him right? Did he say Gina didn't want to come home? Why hadn't someone asked my permission?*

I ran to the telephone, but Frank stopped me.

"Hey, why are you so upset? Do you have something against my family?"

The heated exchange of words started, and turned into an all-out verbal brawl.

I didn't care if he thought I was jealous of his and Gina's relationship or not. I only wanted my little girl back. One recurring thought went through my mind—*Frank would take Gina, and I'd never see her again.*

Only a few days before when I'd talked to her, Gina had said she missed me and couldn't wait to see me.

That night, I couldn't sleep; I knew I had to get Gina. Frank was up to something, and I knew I had to make a move and make it quickly. Questions pounded my brain: "How can I get my daughter back without warning them I was coming? What did Frank tell them?" I loved his family, but I was uncomfortable with Gina being there, at least the way he had misled me.

I decided to call her. I needed to hear her voice and know she was all right. When my sister-in-law answered, I spoke to her nicely, and then asked to speak to Gina.

"Gina's outside," she said. "I don't want to bother her, but she's fine."

I spoke calmly. "It's important I talk to Gina." In a minute, I heard her voice, sweet and clear.

"I thought you were coming to get me," she said.

"I'll see you soon, baby, don't you worry. You have a good time. I miss you, and you know how much I love you."

A weird thought crossed my mind. *Will I ever see her again?*

I made up my mind. *I will get my child!* No matter what I had to do, Gina would see me as soon as I could get to North Carolina.

I called my mother to tell her I was going out of town. "Don't go alone," she begged. She was concerned about my frame of mind and encouraged my sister to go with me.

I became discouraged when I learned Amtrak didn't go to the town where they lived. I would have to travel to another town, get on a bus, and then travel another thirty miles before I reached my destination. I packed only enough clothes for overnight, because my plan was to get Gina and come right back home.

From the start, everything seemed to go against us. First the train was late, and by the time we finally arrived in North Carolina, we missed the connecting bus. When we found someone who could answer our questions about the bus schedule, we discovered that the next bus wasn't due until the next morning.

My sister and I found ourselves stranded in a strange town and had no choice but to sit on a bench outside of a gas station until the next morning. We were in a very small town where everyone watched out for everyone else. We felt safe because the men there reminded us of our uncles and cousins. Someone offered to buy us dinner, but we refused. An older man said we could stay at his house, and he wouldn't come near us. Although he seemed like a man we could trust, we didn't accept his offer. After calling our mother several times about our dilemma, we took turns sleeping on the bench until the bus station opened the next morning.

I became anxious because of all the delays. I just wanted to see my daughter. While we waited for the bus to take us to our destination, another bus arrived. The bus driver said he could take us to the next largest city, which was in South Carolina, because the connection would be closer to where we needed to be.

I felt hysteria creeping in, but I knew I had to stay calm. I was tired, hungry, and running out of money. Only God kept my mind straight. The delays and the waiting were almost too much for me. We hadn't planned to spend extra money for another bus. I still needed to purchase Gina's ticket back home, and I knew I needed enough money for her food.

Lord, please help me. I am so tired. Please let me see my child. I've come so far, and I can't believe all of these detours are part of Your plan.

No sooner than I'd said the prayer, the announcement came that our bus was waiting. My spirit was calm, and I was at peace. I fell asleep as soon as I got seated. I would soon see Gina.

After we reached our destination, my sister retrieved our luggage, and I phoned my sister-in-law.

"I'm at the bus station, and I need a ride to your place. When you come, could you bring Gina?" She was surprised, and said she would meet me as soon as possible.

When the car pulled up, she and my brother-in-law greeted us. I felt as if hummingbirds were darting around in my stomach, but I acted like nothing was wrong. I would finally hold my daughter in my arms. I vowed this would never happen again. I would never let her out of my sight for long, especially when she was with her father. When Gina jumped from the car and raced toward me, I warmly embraced her. *I don't want to ever let you go.*

"Why didn't you come to see me, Mommy?" she asked. "I missed you a lot!" Gina's impish smile made me grin.

We all remained quiet on the ride back to the house. When we arrived, I saw boxes stacked in the corner of a bedroom with Gina's name on them. I opened one box and was shocked to see all her clothes from New York. I noticed the return address was written in Frank's handwriting. My stomach lurched. I had been at home a week without even noticing Gina's clothes were missing.

A thought settled in my brain—*Frank never intended to bring her back.*

How can he do this to me? Doesn't he know I will fight for my daughter, or did he plan to do away with me? For years he had threatened to take Gina from me, and now he had carried out his threat.

What other threat will he fulfill? What if he. . .

I couldn't dwell on the "what ifs." Right now, I had to concentrate on how to explain my arrival in North Carolina. I had to pretend that everything was fine. I took a deep breath and tried to look as relaxed and carefree as possible.

Sitting at the kitchen table, I said, "You don't know how much I missed Gina. We have things planned with her school back in New York, and I have to get home so she doesn't miss anything. I guess Frank forgot about our plans."

I didn't like stretching the truth, but I knew I wouldn't be comfortable until we were seated on the train the next morning, and on our way back home.

I know Frank's sister didn't understand our rush, but we had to leave as soon as possible. Frank was on a trip and wouldn't return for a few days. That gave me the time I needed to get Gina home.

When we boarded the bus, Gina couldn't stop talking.

"What did you do while I was gone?" she asked. "Did you make chocolate chip cookies?" "Did you miss me?" "Oh Mommy, I met a nice little girl on the train when Daddy and I rode it. We even took pictures."

When we finally transferred from the bus to the train, I began to relax. I called my family to let them know I was okay. I could tell by the lilt in my mother's voice that she could hardly wait to see Gina.

When we pulled into New York, an awful thought bore down on me—*I would have to deal with Frank.* I didn't care what he said—I had to bring my daughter home.

When I returned home, the apartment was still in turmoil. I had left in a hurry, and I could tell by the disarray that Frank hadn't been home. That meant he could walk in the door at any time. I quickly cleaned the apartment, because I didn't have the strength to fight, and I didn't want to give him any excuses to fight. I had only been gone three days, yet it felt as if I had been gone a month. I was physically and spiritually drained. I couldn't begin to thank God enough for keeping us safe.

When I heard the key turn in the lock, I knew Frank wouldn't be happy. I had to make him realize that there was no way he could ever take Gina from me. I vowed I would always protect her and nothing could make me break my vow.

Before Frank got home, I told Gina she could play a game and surprise him when he arrived. She hid in the closet, planning to jump out when he walked past. She was so excited about seeing him.

When Frank shoved the door open, I could tell he had already talked to his family. He came toward me, and Gina jumped out of the closet and yelled, "Surprise, Daddy! Did you miss me?"

He played the part of a good father. "I missed you so much that I couldn't sleep. I'm so glad to see you home. Now go play in your room, Gina." Then he calmly shut the door.

The way he walked toward me screamed—*Danger!* He began pounding the air with balled-up fists, and as soon as he reached me, he began hitting my arms and face.

"You hurt my sister! What's the matter with you?" he said, still throwing punches.

It became one of the worst fights we ever had. He picked up a lamp and threw it at me; in fact, he threw anything he could get his hands on.

He lunged at me, and we both hit the floor hard. He kept punching and screaming.

You will not kill me! God has not brought me through this just for me to die!

I fought back with everything that was in me. *I will survive! I will survive to raise my child. Lord, are You there?*

All of a sudden, Frank stopped hitting me. He simply got up and walked out of the apartment without saying a word. From my peripheral vision, I saw a black shadow disappear around a corner of the dining room. *It wasn't my imagination; something was really there .Was the presence a warning to me that my life was about to end?*

While I sat there in the floor thinking about dying, I saw the black shadow again, and I became angry.

Who do you think you are? You can't intrude into my life!

There had been something evil in my apartment, and I thought I couldn't fight it. Then, I bowed my head and prayed, "Father, I pray by the power of Jesus' name that You, and only You, live in this place. I pray You protect Gina and me; keep the Evil One from harming either of us. Lord, I trust You to fight our battles. Like you say in Your Word—*the battle is Yours.* We trust You in this; in everything. I thank You, Lord, that You hear my prayer."

The prayer almost wrung everything out of me. My forehead beaded with sweat. Even though my head pounded and my body ached from the beating, I would trust God in all things.

The presence always seemed to show up whenever Frank went into a rage. I thank God that it couldn't stay when I prayed. All I had to do was pray and keep my mind on God. That's how I would conquer it. *I refuse to be defeated!* God had given me the power to tread on serpents! His power could conquer anything in this world. I had no reason to fear.

I will see my daughter grow up, graduate from college, get married, and have children. It will happen!

When I began to think about life again, and not be fearful, the figure disappeared. It was amazing. I knew how to fight it. I couldn't give into those defeatist feelings. Most of all, I prayed. Prayer has so much power, and I didn't use it. When I prayed, nothing could harm me! It didn't have to be a long prayer with fancy words; it just had to be sincere and come from within my heart.

Prayer is part of my armor; the armor that God has provided for all believers. "Put on the full armor of God so that you can take your stand against the devil's schemes" (Eph. 6:11-18, NIV).

When I went to bed that night following the beating, I knew Gina and I would be all right. I didn't know what would happen, but I knew we would make it. I felt as if I could face any situation and win. God was truly giving me strength for what was about to happen.

When I woke up the next morning, I decided to visit a pastor I knew. I took my marriage vows seriously, and I wanted to get counseling, knowing I would receive the right answer.

In the past, I'd been told that God didn't allow divorce, and I needed to be submissive as the Bible said. I couldn't believe God wanted me to stay in an abusive relationship. Some people had said I needed to be more understanding because my husband was the head of the household.

For me to learn the truth, I made an appointment and met a pastor in his office. Immediately after I walked into his office, the man reached behind me and locked the door.

At first, I thought he locked the door so we wouldn't be disturbed while we spoke. Then, I noticed the twisted smile on his face, and it frightened me. When he moved closer to me, I felt not only fear, but disgust.

He's making a pass at me! What's wrong with him? He's a pastor!

He shoved me against the door and kissed me.

Is this my fault? Am I causing all of this?

My beating the previous night seemed distant.

Oh, if only the floor would open up and swallow me. This can't be happening.

He tried to put his hands on me, and I pushed them away. Then he tried to kiss me again. He pinned me against the office door, and I tried to unlock it, but because of the way I was positioned, I couldn't reach the lock.

I need someone to listen to me! If I can't tell this pastor, then who can I tell?

"Leave me alone," I said, pushing him away. I could hardly speak and my voice didn't sound like me.

"All I want to know is what to do about my husband. He beats me almost every chance he gets, and I'm afraid next time he might kill me." While I talked, I edged closer to the door until I could feel the lock behind me.

I continued. "My marriage vows are important, and I'm confused. I know God didn't put me in this world to be abused. I've heard so many different versions of scripture that I'm not sure what to do."

I began to cry. Hopefully, it would catch the man off guard, and he would forget what he was trying to do and retreat into his ministerial position. "What can I do? Where can I go?"

"Don't worry," he said, "part of your vows says, 'Til death do us part,' which applies in this case because the love has died." I was a free woman! Finally, behind my back, my fingers traced the lock, and I unlocked it. I turned and raced from his office. *Who can I trust if I can't trust a man of God? I don't know if I can ever trust anyone again.* I left his office that day feeling dirty.

When I was at my lowest, I heard that familiar voice again saying, "I'll never leave you, nor forsake you." I knew I would never turn away from God. I buried what happened deep inside, along with the other pain and heartache I felt. I would forget what happened and attend church the next day. I couldn't stop attending; I needed to be in the house of the Lord. I needed something, or someone, to hold on to; someone I trusted.

In my mind, I kept hearing Frank's voice, "I told you so. You should have listened to me."

Gina kept me going. She needed me. I had to press on. At home, I took a shower, washing away the unpleasant memory.

Afterwards, at three o'clock, I waited in front of the school for Gina.

I put on my happy smile as I sat on a bench, waiting. One of the parents came over to say how well the children were doing in school. She began to tell me how blessed I was to have such a wonderful husband.

"Girl, you caught a good one. He is such a loving husband. If I were you, I'd watch out 'cause some of those single mothers are eyeing him."

I wanted to laugh in her face, but didn't. The Devil truly is deceitful. He can blind the eyes of people so they will see only a deceptive light. The Bible warns us of the deception. "For such men are false apostles, deceitful workmen, masquerading as apostles of Christ. And no wonder, for Satan himself masquerades as an angel of light " (2 Cor.11:13, 14, NIV). Unfortunately, I had never heard of the scripture.

When I first met Frank I remember thinking how handsome he was. He had hazel eyes and was always immaculately dressed. *I was blinded by the wrong light!*

Gina ran out of school toward me. She sensed something wrong and grabbed my hand.

"I'm fine, Gina."

"I don't want to share you anymore," she said. We walked to the bus stop, and she added, "Mommy, everything will be all right."

While on the bus, I began to think. If I let Gina have too much fun, Frank always reacted violently. How could I allow him to do this to us? I was tired of the whole thing and made up my mind to confront him.

The more I thought about it, the angrier I became. When he arrived home that night, I felt anger rising up in me. I began slamming things around because I wanted him to ask me what was wrong. I had already fed Gina and sent her to her room. I was ready for whatever happened.

This night I determined I would be the last one standing. No matter what I had to do to him, he would not win this one, even if it meant taking his life. I would plead temporary insanity.

The Devil tries to overtake any situation. He knows that if I had killed Frank, it would mean that I committed murder and would not be allowed to enter heaven unless I repented. The Bible says, "Outside are the dogs, those who practice magic arts, the sexually immoral, the murderers, the idolaters and everyone who loves and practices falsehood" (Rev. 22: 15, NIV).

I had no right to take a life, but it didn't matter anymore. To me, his life was useless. The world would be better off without him. That's how sin starts. It begins as a thought, and if we continue to dwell on it, we will act. We don't need to keep those things in our hearts and allow them to invade the Holy Spirit's space.

However, all I thought about was that Frank had to die so I could live. I knew it wouldn't take long for a fight to begin. So I started. All I had to do was stare at him.

Pretty soon he yelled, "What the h… are you looking at?"

"Dirt!" I said. Anger is a strong emotion. It can make you do things you normally would never do.

This time I lunged for him, grabbing him around his neck, trying to choke the life out of him. I scratched, bit, and kicked. All the years of pain surfaced together with all the memories of what he'd done to me. I was out of control. I pounded him with my fists. I had strength I didn't know I had, but he was stronger and pinned me down, laughing. His face seemed to change. He began slapping me and then decided to satisfy his sexual desire. His laugh hurt my ears, and it seemed to penetrate every ounce of space in the apartment.

The punches and biting and scratching continued. I couldn't feel anything anymore, and the ringing in my head just seemed to get louder. I saw blood on the floor, and through a haze, realized it was mine. Thank God, Gina slept through it. When Frank had enough, he left. I crawled to the bathroom, vomiting and gagging. I soaked myself in the tub and rinsed the blood off me. Then I dried myself off and crawled into bed.

I will never get away! I'm in this for life! There was no one to talk to; no one to go to. I had lost a lot of blood, and I was weak, but I refused to wake Gina up so I could go to the hospital. I had healed before; I would heal again.

Later, I sat in the big chair that I often prayed in, and tried to understand why God allowed Frank to destroy me.

I am trapped like an animal. Why, Lord? Why won't You get rid of him? Please God, help me. Tell me what to do.

Although I didn't hear an answer, I felt peace envelope me.

Was this what it was like to die? How could I feel this amazing peace? I now know what it's like to be in the middle of a storm and feel perfect peace.

I was confident things would be fine. I wouldn't die, and Gina wouldn't be raised by someone else, and we *would* be happy.

With cuts, scratches, and bruises all over me, I couldn't go to work the next day. Frank took Gina to school. I couldn't show myself. People would start asking questions, and I wouldn't answer. On the other hand, I couldn't keep calling in sick. I knew I would either lose my job, or I'd have to change jobs again. It was getting harder to hide the scrapes and bruises.

How many times could I explain my accidents? I had "walked into doorways," "fell down the steps," and "tripped on something" too many times. It was so frequent that people thought I was clumsy. I let them think it.

As I cleaned the house that day, I began to make a plan. Maybe I could leave New York. We needed to go someplace where he would never find us. When it was safe, I would call my family and let them know where we were. I had an education, Gina easily made friends, and we would be happy.

I refused to live like this any longer. I knew Frank would never leave me, and one day, he would succeed in killing me. If the beatings didn't kill me, the irreparable harm done to my physical body, inside and out, would. I had so much surgery that my body looked like a road map. Each scar represented a different *"state"* Frank had been in. I felt I would carry those scars forever.

How can I escape, Lord? I don't know how to start over. I have to get out. Are you listening, Lord? I have to get away from Frank.

Escaping would mean changing our way of life, and Gina was doing very well in school. Her grades were always above average, and she seemed to be happy, in spite of all that was going on. I tried to keep her happy by showering her with all the love I possibly could. I hugged her and told her how very much I loved her. I made up my mind that no matter what she needed, she would have it. *How can I pull up roots and take her from her family and friends? Could she adjust to a new life? Could I? Where would we go?*

The only way I could get out of my situation was to keep praying, keep talking to God. All day, I kept feeling as though God was waiting for me to make a move. When I arrived home that night, for no apparent reason, Frank was in one of his rages.

He seemed restless and nervous, as if he were waiting for someone. When the phone rang, he jumped, and when someone walked down our hall, he looked through the peephole.

"What's wrong?" I finally asked.

He began screaming at me, then pushed me aside and left the apartment. Gina heard his scream and came out of her room. When she saw he'd left, she gave me a warm hug and kissed my cheek.

A strange calmness washed over me, and I went into the living room, got down on my knees and began to talk to God like I'd never talked to Him before.

"Father, I am so sorry. I have let You down. I know I haven't been reading Your Word or praying like I should. Please, God, I don't understand why I'm going through this or why I'm being punished . . ." Tears wet my face. I wiped them with my hand. "I love You so much, Lord, in spite of everything I've experienced. Please, God, provide a way out for me."

It's hard to explain, but as I prayed, I felt God standing there and soothing me. When the tears fell like rain, it was as though He reached out and wiped them away.

The last thing I said was, "I am ready to do Your will, not mine."

When I got off my knees, I went into my bedroom and lay down, still feeling His presence. I was so calm that I fell asleep.

I heard the sound of someone singing, "Peace be still." Whoever it was, they seemed to be right in the bedroom with me. I could not discern whether it was male or female, but it was so soothing. Then, I saw a bright light coming down the hallway of our apartment. I was not afraid, and I knew that the end of my trial was near. The light came closer, and I could feel its warmth. Just as it got really near, I closed my eyes because of its brightness. When I opened my eyes again, everything returned to normal. The dream gave me a sense of security and of peace like I'd never experienced. Even the apartment seemed peaceful.

CHAPTER XVI

On April 2, 1979, I awakened with a start, realizing the house was too quiet. Maybe Frank hadn't come home. Then, I heard the sound of the shower.

He's home all right, I thought. *Lord, I know you heard my prayer last night, and I put all my trust in You.*

It was late, and Gina had a treat ahead of her—one of the parents had offered to drive her to school.

I went in to wake Gina up and was surprised to see how sound asleep she was. I called to her very quietly, "Gina, it's time to wake up. It's late; we must have overslept."

She woke up smiling, just like when she was a baby. "Hi Mommy!"

I turned from her and hollered at my husband. "Frank, how long are you going to be in the shower?" His mumbling was indiscernible. I listened at the door. It almost sounded as though he were speaking a foreign language.

When Frank walked out of the bathroom, he shot me an odd look.

"Frank, what's wrong?" He didn't answer.

I rushed Gina into the bathroom and gave her a quick bath and hurried her into her room to put on her school uniform. Noticing her rumpled hair, I said, "Gina, come in my room. I want to fix your hair."

The noise behind me made me turn quickly. When I looked, Frank had a strange smile on his face.

"Frank, what's wrong? Why are you looking at me like that?" He had one hand behind his back and when he pulled it out, he held the gun I thought he'd disposed of years before. Without a word, he held the gun to my head. He looked over his shoulder as though he were awaiting instructions from an unseen being.

"It's over, baby," he said. "This is for you and what you've done to me."

I looked into his eyes, and I knew this was the turning point.

Please, God, don't let Gina see me die like this. Let me get her out of the house. Please . . ."

Gina was almost eight years old, and I didn't want her to spend the rest of her life remembering my dying in front of her.

Just the night before, I had poured out my heart to God and asked for His help. I believed with all my heart that I would not be harmed. I had felt His presence.

Oh, Lord, I know you are with me. You won't let me die. Father, protect me. What about my baby? What will happen to her?

My mother's love poured out, and as usual, Gina sensed my distress. She crawled into my lap and gazed into my eyes. I hugged her, and then tried to put her down, but she wouldn't turn loose of me. It was as if she knew that if she stayed in my lap, nothing would happen. Her father would never hurt her.

I turned Gina around so that she faced me and had her back to her father.

I want her face to be the last thing I see, and if she has to be here, I pray the Lord wipes this memory from her.

Frank looked over his shoulder again as if he were listening to someone. Then he shook his head. Slowly, it came to me that I was in a fight for my soul. It was the age-old fight between God and Satan, and I knew who would win. God had already told me He would fight my battles. I had to believe and trust Him. I had experienced so much, but I knew God would never leave me. He promised He wouldn't. Frank put the gun to my head, and I knew he was going to pull the trigger.

The phone jangled. I tried to take it off the hook, hoping the person on the other end would hear all the commotion. Maybe if they heard voices, I reasoned, they would figure out that I was in trouble. But Frank stopped me.

I didn't dare provoke him, and I quickly pulled my hand away from the telephone. The caller called again and Frank said, "You better not answer." He was determined to finish the job he'd started. He demanded that Gina get off my lap, but she refused.

I held my breath. Frank was really going to shoot me.

Don't! I have too much to live for. Oh, God, I want to live!

Frank pulled the trigger and I heard the click. It seemed to echo throughout the room, but nothing happened. He looked behind him, and cocked his head as if he were still listening to someone. He nodded. Then he squinted his eyes and looked directly at me. He pulled the trigger. Again.

God was still in charge! I suddenly felt a calmness; a stillness within my spirit. I looked into Frank's eyes and this time, I smiled! I knew I would be all right. In my living room, a spiritual battle for my life had taken place. God won, just as I knew He would. The gun was full of bullets, but they never discharged!

Frank looked at Gina, then at me. "Take her to school." He walked out the door. Just like that, it was over.

Despite being in shock, I quickly dressed Gina. "Come on, precious. Put on your jacket so I can take you to meet Ms. Tompson." We raced to the elevator and outside the building. Ms. Tompson was still waiting.

"Girl," she said, "I called you, but the phone kept ringing. Are you all right? I was about to leave, but had the feeling I should wait."

"Yes, I'm all right now." I quickly kissed Gina good-bye and went back to the apartment.

I sat on my bed a long time, and then I phoned my mother.

"M-Mom, Frank just put a gun to my head. He tried to kill me. I-I can't seem to think."

"Baby," she said, "are you all right?"

I took a deep breath and said, "Yes."

"Well then, you just go get Gina from school so Frank won't take her. I'm sending your sister to go with you. And call the police."

I didn't remember calling the police, but I must have. They were there in a matter of minutes.

I sat at my kitchen table, and my hands were trembling. "My husband just put a gun to my head. I don't know where he is, but I've got to get my daughter from school. Please find him. I'm pressing charges."

After the police left, I sat there for a few minutes, trying to absorb what had just happened.

My sister's face looked fearful. "Let's get out of here," she said. "We don't know where Frank is, and we don't want to take any chances."

"Are you hungry?" I asked as if nothing was wrong. "Can I fix you some breakfast?" I couldn't get past the denial, and instead fell into a comfortable pattern of hospitality.

"Bonita! Snap out of it. We've got to get out of here. Don't worry about clothes or anything. Let's go!"

I called the school, informed them I was coming to get Gina, and told them they were, under no circumstances, to release her to her father.

I later found out he did try to take her out of school. I walked out of the apartment building, and I nervously looked around to see if Frank was nearby, waiting to do what he had always planned—to kill me.

At the school, I told Gina that we were going to my mother's for a while.

"Sweetheart, we are going to stay with Mama. Won't that be fun? You can play with your cousin and see your aunts all the time."

She seemed excited. "Yes! We're going to stay with Mama!" Her expression changed. "Is Daddy coming too?"

I looked into her big, expressive brown eyes and said, "No honey, not this time, but we'll be just fine."

She smiled and said, "Okay."

We left with only the clothes on our backs, but we were free, and we were alive. That night, I heard Gina crying as she got ready for bed. I had never heard her sob like that before.

"Oh, honey, I'm so sorry you're sad. But we needed to get away from Daddy. Are you afraid he's coming to get us?" I still remember the look on her face and how she stood there like the mature child she was and said, "No, Mommy. I'm afraid you might go back. If you do, Daddy will hurt you worse than before, and I don't want anything to happen to you." I made a promise that we would never return. I kept that promise.

The next few months weren't easy. Frank threatened to kill my family, my friends, and me. I would answer the telephone only to hear him say, "You better come home. I will kill your entire family. Come home, I said!"

The next time he called, he threatened, "You never know where I am. I could be behind you, put the gun to your head and kill you. You think the police can find me? I move around too much." I would leave the house not knowing whether I would return, or if it would be the day he would kill me.

Finally, I couldn't take any more threats, and when he called, my answer to him was, "Stop talking. Just do it!" I heard him gasp on the other end as if someone had punched him. Pretty soon, the threatening phone calls stopped.

He soon changed his tune. "Please come back. I'm sorry. I'll take counseling, I'll do anything. Please, I love you so much." When that didn't work, he called one day to say he was in the hospital, dying. I never went to see him. I didn't believe him, and what's more, I didn't care.

As the result of the beatings, I had three more surgeries after I left Frank, but God healed my body.

Frank stopped calling for two years and when he did call again, it was because he wanted to see Gina. That day, he met her at my mother's house, gave her some money and left. He bragged about his new job. He said he was leaving for Europe to work with some famous movie stars.

He even suggested we join him and start a new life. It was over between us. I had nothing left to give. Love was gone, and I had no more feelings for him. We have not seen him since.

I've heard people say that a victim of abuse will leave an abuser and find another one. Society also says the child of this kind of dysfunctional family would turn out badly and probably be an abuser or marry one.

Frank's family turned against me. Some called to say, "You better go home. Your child is going to be a streetwalker or a dropout." "You'll never amount to anything." "You ruined Frank; he wasn't like that before he married you." "Everything that happened is your entire fault." I only listened with half an ear. I knew better. I was the one who survived.

Gina stayed in school and kept a ninety-eight average through high school. She attended and graduated from an Ivy League college, receiving her Bachelor's degree, and then went on to receive her Master of Divinity.

She is now married to a wonderful man, who is *not* an abuser. They have two beautiful, loving children. She is the first woman pastor in the state we live in and the youngest. She will receive her Ph.D. in a few months.

I have since remarried a man who is *not* an abuser. He is a gentle man who hardly ever raises his voice and when he does, it's not to me. We knew each other for many years before we married. His family lived in the same building where my mother lived.

I am also an ordained minister and have a ministry, Fighting Abuse In The Home (F.A.I.T.H.), which helps those who are in abusive situations. I minister to women who are abused or have been abused. Whenever I am called to preach the Word, I always let the congregation know what I have been through. That is my testimony.

I remember that last night in the apartment when I poured out my heart; my life to God. I said, "Your will; not mine, Lord." That was the beginning of life for me. God is always true to His Word. When He promised to never leave me, He kept that promise. He says: "So is my word that goes out from my mouth: It will not return to me empty, but will accomplish what I desire and achieve the purpose for which I sent it" (Isaiah 55:11, NIV).

It is time for me to do the work for which God prepared me. I am not saying that God creates these circumstances so we will do what He wants. We all have free will, meaning that we have a choice. I made a bad choice when I married Frank. God did not tell me to marry him. I had many warnings by friends and family, but I made the choice to marry him. Although I made the wrong choice, I am able to use my bad choices as an example.

I praise God for my daughter who is a product of that marriage. She is truly a blessing, and I am so proud of her. She never looked at herself as a product of a broken marriage. She is a survivor and has a calling to minister to youth believing that no child should be shoved aside; every child has a right to be happy, safe and to make something of themselves.

If it hadn't been for Gina, I probably would have given up on myself, and on life. When she was born, when God gave me this gift,

I knew I had to make sure she had whatever she needed. She needed a mother. She also needed a good father-figure; unfortunately, that did not happen in Frank. Still, Gina had a family that stood behind her in all her decisions.

Despite all that happened, she knew she was loved. She had the freedom to talk to me about anything. The doors of communication were always open. When she needed a hug, she got it; when she needed to be held; she got it, and when she just wanted someone to listen, she received that too.

I never spoke against her father in her presence, because he was still her father. Anything she felt against him was because of his own actions. It wasn't necessary to fill her with negativity. She knew what was going on. My job was to make sure she knew that she was loved and to speak positive things to her and tell her about God.

There are thousands of children who live in abusive households, and the numbers are rising instead of falling. Many of these children never make it out of the abuse, and eventually they are killed. Several children go to school every day only to come home and be physically and mentally abused. We have a responsibility to our children. They can't protect themselves, so we have to step in and help them. Don't keep silent if you have any suspicions of domestic abuse or child abuse. I have included resource information as well as symptoms to look for in abused persons.

I praise God that I got out. I never could have done it alone. He is my protector, my Rock, my strength, and the One from whom all blessings flow. Yes, I am blessed. What the devil meant for evil, God turned around for good. I have come out of the wilderness of domestic violence into the Promised Land of ministry.

To God be the glory!

"She said to herself, 'If I only touch his cloak, I will be healed.' Jesus turned and saw her. 'Take heart, daughter,' he said, 'your faith has healed you.' And the woman was healed from that moment"(Matt.9:21, 22, NIV).

Amen.

INFORMATION

STAGES OF VIOLENCE

The cycle of violence is a predictable pattern that research has linked with violent relationships. The cycle has three stages:

- Tension-Building
- Explosion
- Honeymoon.

This cycle varies in timing for individual relationships. Denial is a key factor that keeps both partners tightly bound in this vicious cycle. This denial must be broken. In order to do so, some intervention must be sought.....counseling, support groups, or separation if the other means fail. When both partners seek help individually, there is hope that the cycle of violence will be broken.

Tension-Building

During this stage, the person being abused reports feeling as though they are "walking on egg shells," careful not to upset or make angry the abuser. The belief is that by not upsetting the abuser, they can prevent or control the violence. The abuser blames those around for the problems they are facing, they become more possessive, jealous and increasingly lose control.

Explosion

Violence occurs. It may take the form of verbal, emotional/psychological, physical, or sexual abuse (or a combination of these). Any incident (often insignificant incidents) may trigger the abuse. Chemical usage may or may not be involved along with the abuse. The abuser feels "relieved" after the explosion, often appearing calm. However, the abused individual may be extremely upset, confused, or numb, along with the physical and emotional pain. If police are called and arrive at the scene at this time, the behavior of the person that was abused is mistakenly questioned because they MAY appear out of control and the abuser calm. (Hence the need for education and awareness for officers).

Honeymoon

During this phase, the abuser promises never to hurt his partner again, promises to seek help, and may feel guilt or remorse. But often these are attempts to keep their partner. Too often, the abuser continues to blame their partner for the violence, and will make them feel guilty and responsible for their behavior. The abused person believes that their partner will change during this time frame – they see the person they originally fell in love with.

Denial

As long as denial exists for either partner, the violence will continue.

Adapted from: "Cycle of Violence" Theory – Lenore Walker

CYCLE OF VIOLENCE

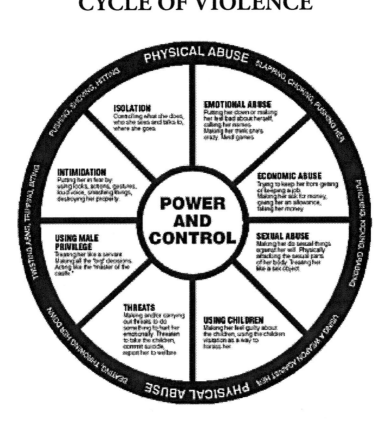

Bonita Chase

CYCLE OF NONVIOLENCE

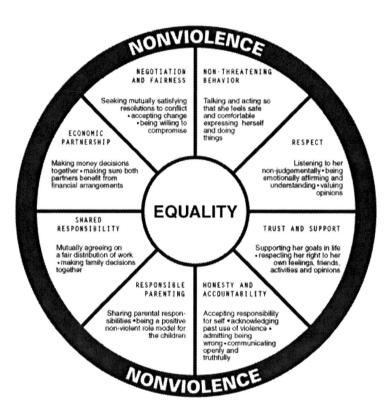

112

RADAR

Remember to ask routinely about violence.

Ask questions. "At any time, has your partner hit, kicked, or otherwise hurt or frightened you?" Interview patients in private at all times.

Document findings. Information about suspected domestic violence in a patient's chart can be used in court cases.

Assess patients' safety. Is it safe to return home? Find out if there are any weapons; are children in danger; is the violence escalating.

Review options. Let patient know where there is help. Tell them about shelters, support groups and legal advocates.

Massachusets College of Emergency Physicians

Safety Plan

If you are still in the relationship:

- Think of a safe place to go if an argument occurs - avoid rooms with no exits (bathroom), or rooms with weapons (kitchen).
- Think about and make a list of safe people to contact.
- Keep change with you at all times.
- Memorize all important numbers.
- Establish a "code word" or "sign" so that family, friends, teachers or co-workers know when to call for help.
- Think about what you will say to your partner if he\she becomes violent.

Remember, you have the right to live without fear and violence.

If you have left the relationship:

- Change your phone number.
- Screen calls.
- Save and document all contacts, messages, injuries or other incidents involving the batterer.
- Change locks, if the batterer has a key.
- Avoid staying alone.

- Plan how to get away if confronted by an abusive partner.
- If you have to meet your partner, do it in a public place.
- Vary your routine.
- Notify school and work contacts.
- Call a shelter for battered women.

If you leave the relationship or are thinking of leaving, you should take important papers and documents with you to enable you to apply for benefits or take legal action.

Important papers you should take include social security cards and birth certificates for you and your children, your marriage license, leases or deeds in your name or both yours and your partner's names, your checkbook, your charge cards, bank statements and charge account statements, insurance policies, proof of income for you and your spouse (pay stubs or W-2's), and any documentation of past incidents of abuse (photos, police reports, medical records, etc.)

National Coalition Against Domestic Violence (www.ncadv.org)

My Personal Safety Plan – Worksheet

The following steps are my plan for increasing my safety and preparing to protect myself in case of further abuse.

Although I can't control my abuser's violence, I do have a choice about how I respond and how I get to safety. I will decide for myself if and when I will tell others that I have been abused, or that I am still at risk. Friends, family and co-workers can help protect me, if they know what is happening, and what they can do to help.

To increase my safety, I can do some or all of the following:

1. When I have to talk to my abuser in person, I can:

2. When I talk to my abuser on the phone, I can:

3. I will make up a "code word" for my family, co-workers, or friends, so they know when to call for help for me. My code word is:

4. When I feel a fight coming on, I will try to move to a place that is lowest risk for getting hurt such as: or (at work):or: (at home) (in public)

5. I can tell my family, co-workers, boss, or a friend about my situation. I feel safe telling:

6. I can use an answering machine or ask my co-workers, friends or other family members to screen my calls and visitors. I have the right to not receive harassing phone calls. I can ask:to help screen (home) (work) my phone calls.

7. I can keep change for phone calls with me at all times. I can call any of the following people for assistance or support if necessary and can ask them to call the police if they see my abuser bothering me. friend: relative: co-worker: counselor: shelter: other:

8. When leaving work I can:

9. When walking, riding or driving home, if problems occur, I can:

10. I can attend a support group for women who have been abused. Support groups are held: at:

11. Telephone Numbers I Need to Know: Police/Sheriffs Department: Probation Officer: Domestic Violence/Sexual Assault Program: Counselor: Clergy Person: Attorney: Other:

National Coalition Against Domestic Violence (www.ncadv.org)

Protecting Your Identity

Identity theft is rampant in the United States. Survivors of domestic violence must take extra precautions to proect themselves from abusers who use identity as a means of power and control. Abusers may use survivors' credit cards without their permission, open fradulent new credit cards in survivors' names (ultimately ruining their credit) or open credit cards in children's names. Misuse of survivors' social security numbers is also common in the context of domestic violence. Abusers may fradulently use survivors' social security numbers to stalk, harass or threaten survivors. Read more to learn how to protect yourself if you are experiencing this type of abuse.

Survivors experiencing abuse should contact their local domestic violence program for immediate support. Check your local yellow pages or call the National Domestic Violence Hotline (operated by the Texas Council on Family Violence) at 1-800-799-SAFE to be connected to the program in your area.

Steps to Take to Protect Your Identity

Relocate. Moving across town, across the state or across the country puts physical distance between you and the abuser. Be sure to obtain an unlisted phone number and be aware of the Full Faith and Credit provisions in your restraining order, which make the order valid when you travel to another state or tribal jurisdiction.

Apply to the address confidentiality program in your state. These types of programs allow individuals who have experienced domestic violence, sexual assault, stalking or other types of crime to receive mail at a confidential address, while keeping their actual address undisclosed. Rules and eligibility vary from state to state. Click here to see a list of address confidentiality programs in states across the country.

Open a post office box to receive mail. Abusers may be able to open fraudulent credit cards by responding to credit card offers received in the mail. A post office box may prevent this if only you have access to it. Be wary of the confidentiality policies of non-government post office box centers such as Mail Boxes, Etc…and the fact that it may not be possible to remain anonymous in rural towns while accessing the post office.

Protect your incoming and outgoing mail. Shred all credit card offers that come in the mail along with other documents that have your name, address and/or social security number on them. Mail bills and other sensitive documents directly from the post office instead of from the mailbox on your porch or at the end of your driveway. Call 1-800-5OPT-OUT to stop receiving credit card offers in the mail.

Guard your social security number. Do not use your social security number as a general ID, PIN or password. Request to have your social security number removed from documents you receive in the mail and ID cards for health insurance, driving, work, etc… Click here to read about changing your social security number.

Check your credit report. The best way to determine if someone has committed fraud against you is to check your credit report with all three credit bureaus at least once per year. Visit www.annualcreditreport.com to obtain a free yearly credit report. You can also make a request to have a fraud alert placed on your credit report. Click here to find out how to contact the credit bureaus.

Report suspected fraud. Contact local law enforcement if you know of or suspect fraud and ask to file a report. Check and/or close accounts you believe have been tampered. File a report with the Federal Trade Commission at 1-877-ID-THEFT and the Social Security

Administration Fraud Hotline at 1-800-269-0271. File copies of police reports with credit bureaus.

Protect information you give out. Never give any identifying information over the phone or through email or the internet unless you initiated the call or have verification that the website or email communication is secure.

Other Helpful Websites:

Privacy Rights Clearinghouse: Nonprofit Consumer Information and Advocacy Organization: www.privacyrights.org

Identity Theft Resource Center: www.idtheftcenter.org

Federal Trade Commission: www.consumer.gov/idtheft/

The National Center for Victims of Crime: www.ncvc.org

US Department of Justice: www.usdoj.gov/criminal/fraud/idtheft.html

State Coalition List

Alabama Coalition Against Domestic Violence
P. O. Box 4762 - Montgomery, AL 36101
(334) 832-4842 Fax: (334) 832-4803 - (800) 650-6522 Hotline
Website: www.acadv.org Email: acadv@acadv.org

Alaska Network on Domestic and Sexual Violence
130 Seward Street, Room 209 - Juneau, AK 99801
(907) 586-3650 Fax: (907) 463-4493 Website: www.andvsa.org

Arizona Coalition Against Domestic Violence
100 W. Camelback, #109 - Phoenix, AZ 85013
(602) 279-2900 Fax: (602) 279-2980 (800) 782-6400 Nationwide
Website: www.azcadv.org
Email: acadv@azadv.org

Arkansas Coalition Against Domestic Violence
1401 W. Capitol Avenue, Suite 170 - Little Rock, AR 72201
(501) 907-5612 Fax: (501) 907-5618 (800) 269-4668 Nationwide
Website: www.domesticpeace.com Email: kbangert@domesticpeace.com

California Partnership to End Domestic Violence
P. O. Box 1798 - Sacramento, CA 95812
(916) 444-7163 Fax: (916) 444-7165 (800) 524-4765 Nationwide
Website: www.cpedv.org
Email: info@cpedv.org

Colorado Coalition Against Domestic Violence
P. O. Box 18902 - Denver, CO 80218
(303) 831-9632 Fax: (303) 832-7067 (888) 788-7091 Website: www.
ccadv.org

Connecticut Coalition Against Domestic Violence
90 Pitkin Street East Hartford, CT 06108
(860) 282-7899 Fax: (860) 282-7892 (800) 281-1481 In State
(888) 774-2900 In State DV Hotline Website: www.ctcadv.org
Email: info@ctcadv.org

Delaware Coalition Against Domestic Violence
100 W. 10th Street, #703 Wilmington, DE 19801
(302) 658-2958 Fax: (302) 658-5049 (800) 701-0456
StatewideWebsite: www.dcadv.org
Email: dcadv@dcadv.org

DC Coalition Against Domestic Violence
1718 P Street, Suite T-6 Washington, DC 20036
(202) 299-1181 Fax: (202) 299-1193 Website: www.dccadv.org
Email: help@dccadv.org

Florida Coalition Against Domestic Violence
425 Office Plaza Tallahassee, FL 32301
(850) 425-2749 Fax: (850) 425-3091 (850) 621-4202 TDD (800)
500-1119 In State
Website: www.fcadv.org

Georgia Coalition Against Domestic Violence
3420 Norman Berry Drive, #280 Atlanta, GA 30354
(404) 209-0280 Fax: (404) 766-3800 Website: www.gcadv.org

Hawaii State Coalition Against Domestic Violence
716 Umi Street, Suite 210 Honolulu, HI 96819-2337
(808) 832-9316 Fax: (808) 841-6028 Website: www.hscadv.org

Idaho Coalition Against Sexual & Domestic Violence
815 Park Boulevard, #140 Boise, ID 83712
(208) 384-0419 Fax: (208) 331-0687 (888) 293-6118 Nationwide
Website: www.idvsa.org Email: domvio@mindspring.com

Illinois Coalition Against Domestic Violence
801 S. 11th Street Springfield, IL 62703
(217) 789-2830 Fax: (217) 789-1939 Website: www.ilcadv.org
Email: ilcadv@ilcadv.org

Indiana Coalition Against Domestic Violence
1915 W. 18th Street Indianapolis, IN 46202
(317) 917-3685 Fax: (317) 917-3695 (800) 332-7385 In State
Website: www.violenceresource.org Email: icadv@violenceresource.org

Iowa Coalition against Domestic Violence
515 28th Street, #104 Des Moines, IA 50312
(515) 244-8028 Fax: (515) 244-7417 (800) 942-0333 In State Hotline
Website: www.icadv.org

Kansas Coalition against Sexual and Domestic Violence
634 SW Harrison Street Topeka, KS 66603
(785) 232-9784 Fax: (785) 266-1874 Website: www.kcsdv.org
Email: coalition@kcsdv.org

Kentucky Domestic Violence Association
P.O. Box 356 Frankfort, KY 40602
(502) 695-2444 Fax: (502) 695-2488 Website: www.kdva.org

Louisiana Coalition Against Domestic Violence
P.O. Box 77308 Baton Rouge, LA 70879
(225) 752-1296 Fax: (225) 751-8927 Website: www.lcadv.org

Maine Coalition To End Domestic Violence
170 Park Street Bangor, ME 04401
(207) 941-1194 Fax: (207) 941-2327 Website: www.mcedv.org
Email: info@mcedv.org

Maryland Network Against Domestic Violence
6911 Laurel-Bowie Road, #309 Bowie, MD 20715
(301) 352-4574 Fax: (301) 809-0422 (800) 634-3577 Nationwide
Website: www.mnadv.org Email: mnadv@aol.com

Jane Doe, Inc./Massachusetts Coalition Against Sexual Assault and
Domestic Violence
14 Beacon Street, #507 Boston, MA 02108
(617) 248-0922 Fax: (617) 248-0902 TTY/TTD: (617) 263-2200
Website: www.janedoe.org Email: info@janedoe.org

Michigan Coalition against Domestic & Sexual Violence
3893 Okemos Road, #B-2 Okemos, MI 48864
(517) 347-7000 Fax: (517) 347-1377 TTY: (517) 381-8470
Website: www.mcadsv.org Email: general@mcadsv.org

Minnesota Coalition For Battered Women
1821 University Avenue West, #S-112 St. Paul, MN 55104
(651) 646-6177 Fax: (651) 646-1527 Crisis Line: (651) 646-0994
(800) 289-6177 Nationwide Website: www.mcbw.org
Email: mcbw@mcbw.org

Mississippi Coalition Against Domestic Violence
P.O. Box 4703 Jackson, MS 39296
(601) 981-9196 Fax: (601) 981-2501 Website: www.mcadv.org

Missouri Coalition Against Domestic Violence
718 East Capitol Avenue Jefferson City, MO 65101
(573) 634-4161 Fax: (573) 636-3728 Website: www.mocadv.org
Email: mcadv@sockets.net

Montana Coalition Against Domestic & Sexual Violence
P.O. Box 818 Helena, MT 59624
(406) 443-7794 Fax: (406) 443-7818 (888) 404-7794 Nationwide
Website: www.mcadsv.com Email: mcadsv@mt.net

Nebraska Domestic Violence and Sexual Assault Coalition
825 M Street, #404 Lincoln, NE 68508
(402) 476-6256 Fax: (402) 476-6806 (800) 876-6238 In State
Website: www.ndvsac.org Email: info@ndvsac.org

Nevada Network Against Domestic Violence
100 West Grove Street, #315 Reno, NV 89509
(775) 828-1115 Fax: (775) 828-9911 (800) 500-1556 In State
Website: www.nnadv.org

New Hampshire Coalition Against Domestic and Sexual Violence
P.O. Box 353 Concord, NH 03302
(603) 224-8893 Fax: (603) 228-6096 (866) 644-3574 In State
Website: www.nhcadsv.org

New Jersey Coalition for Battered Women
1670 Whitehorse Hamilton Square Trenton, NJ 08690
(609) 584-8107 Fax: (609) 584-9750 (800) 572-7233 In State
Website: www.njcbw.org Email: info@njcbw.org

New Mexico State Coalition Against Domestic Violence
200 Oak NE, #4 Albuquerque, NM 87106
(505) 246-9240 Fax: (505) 246-9434 (800) 773-3645 In State
Website: www.nmcadv.org

New York State Coalition Against Domestic Violence
350 New Scotland Avenue Albany, NY 12054
(518) 482-5464 Fax: (518) 482-3807 (800) 942-6906 English-In State
(800) 942-6908 Spanish-In State
Website: www.nyscadv.org Email: nyscadv@nyscadv.org

North Carolina Coalition Against Domestic Violence
115 Market Street, #400 Durham, NC 27701
(919) 956-9124 Fax: (919) 682-1449 (888) 232-9124 Nation wide
Website: www.nccadv.org

North Dakota Council on Abused Women's Services
418 E. Rosser Avenue, #320 Bismark, ND 58501
(701) 255-6240 Fax: (701) 255-1904 (888) 255-6240 Nationwide
Website: www.ndcaws.org Email: ndcaws@ndcaws.org

Action Ohio Coalition For Battered Women
P.O. Box 15673 Columbus, OH 43215
(614) 221-1255 Fax: (614) 221-6357 (888) 622-9315 In State
Website: www.actionohio.org Email: actionoh@ee.net

Ohio Domestic Violence Network
4807 Evanswood Drive, #201 Columbus, OH 43229
(614) 781-9651 Fax: (614) 781-9652 (800) 934-9840
Website: www.odvn.org Email: info@odvn.org

Oklahoma Coalition Against Domestic Violence and Sexual Assault
3815 N. Sante Fe Ave., Suite 124 Oklahoma City, OK 73118
(405) 524-0700 Fax: (405) 524-0711 Website: www.ocadvsa.org

Oregon Coalition Against Domestic and Sexual Violence
380 SE Spokane Street, #100 Portland, OR 97202
(503) 230-1951 Fax: (503) 230-1973 Website: www.ocadsv.com

Pennsylvania Coalition Against Domestic Violence
6400 Flank Drive, #1300 Harrisburg, PA 17112
(717) 545-6400 Fax: (717) 545-9456 (800) 932-4632 Nationwide
Website: www.pcadv.org

The Office of Women Advocates
Box 11382 Fernandez Juancus Station Santurce, PR 00910
(787) 721-7676 Fax: (787) 725-9248

Rhode Island Coalition Against Domestic Violence
422 Post Road, #202 Warwick, RI 02888
(401) 467-9940 Fax: (401) 467-9943 (800) 494-8100 In State
Website: www.ricadv.org Email: ricadv@ricadv.org

South Carolina Coalition Against Domestic Violence and Sexual
Assault
P.O. Box 7776 Columbia, SC 29202
(803) 256-2900 Fax: (803) 256-1030 (800) 260-9293 Nationwide
Website: www.sccadvasa.org

South Dakota Coalition Against Domestic Violence & Sexual Assault
P.O. Box 141 Pierre, SD 57501
(605) 945-0869 Fax: (605) 945-0870 (800) 572-9196 Nationwide
Website: www.southdakotacoalition.org Email: sdcadvsa@rapidnet.
com

Tennessee Coalition Against Domestic and Sexual Violence
P.O. Box 120972 Nashville, TN 37212
(615) 386-9406 Fax: (615) 383-2967 (800) 289-9018 In State
Website: www.tcadsv.org Email: tcadsv@tcadsv.org

Texas Council On Family Violence
P.O. Box 161810 Austin, TX 78716
(512) 794-1133 Fax: (512) 794-1199 (800) 525-1978 In State
Website: www.tcfv.org

Women's Coalition of St. Croix
Box 2734 Christiansted St. Croix, VI 00822
(340) 773-9272 Fax: (340) 773-9062 Website: www.wcstx.com
Email: wcscstx@attglobal.net

Utah Domestic Violence Council
320 W. 200 South, #270-B Salt Lake City, UT 84101
(801) 521-5544 Fax: (801) 521-5548 Website: www.udvac.org

Vermont Network Against Domestic Violence and Sexual Assault
P.O. Box 405 Montpelier, VT 05601
(802) 223-1302 Fax: (802) 223-6943 Website: www.vtnetwork.org
Email: vtnetwork@vtnetwork.org

Virginians Against Domestic Violence
2850 Sandy Bay Road, #101 Williamsburg, VA 23185
(757) 221-0990 Fax: (757) 229-1553 (800) 838-8238 Nationwide
Website: www.vadv.org Email: vadv@tni.net

Washington State Coalition Against Domestic Violence
101 N. Capitol Way, #302 Olympia, WA 98501
(360) 586-1022 Fax: (360) 586-1024 1402 – 3rd Avenue, #406
Seattle, WA 98101
(206) 389-2515 Fax. (206) 389-2520 (800) 886-2880 In State
Website: www.wscadv.org Email: wscadv@wscadv.org

West Virginia Coalition Against Domestic Violence
4710 Chimney Drive, #A Charleston, WV 25302
(304) 965-3552 Fax: (304) 965-3572 Website: www.wvcadv.org

Wisconsin Coalition Against Domestic Violence
307 S. Paterson Street, #1 Madison, WI 53703
(608) 255-0539 Fax: (608) 255-3560
Website: www.wcadv.org Email: wcadv@wcadv.org

Wyoming Coalition Against Domestic Violence and Sexual Assault
P.O. Box 236 409 South Fourth Street Laramie, WY 82073
(307) 755-5481 Fax: (307) 755-5482 (800) 990-3877 Nationwide
Website: www.wyomingdvsa.org Email: Info@mail.wyomingdvsa.
org

National Coalition Against Domestic Violence (www.ncadv.org)

Other US Organizations

American Bar Association Commission on Domestic Violence
740 - 15th Street NW, Washington, DC 20005
Phone 202-662-1000, Website www.abanet.org/domviol

American Institute on Domestic Violence
2116 Rover Drive, Lake Havasu City, AZ 86403
Phone 928-453-9015, Website www.aidv-usa.com

Amnesty International USA, Women's Human Rights Program
322 Eighth Avenue, New York, NY 10001
Phone 212-633-4292, Website www.amnestyusa.org/women

Asian and Pacific Islander Institute on Domestic Violence
450 Sutter St #600, San Francisco, CA 94108
Phone 415-954-9988 ext. 315, Website www.apiahf.org/apidvinstitute

The Audre Lorde Project
85 S. Oxford Street, Brooklyn, NY 11217
Phone 718-596-0342, Website www.alp.org

The BWJP Criminal Justice Office
2104 Fourth Ave S #B, Minneapolis, MN 55404
Phone 612-824-8768 / 1-800-903-0111 ext. 1

The BWJP Civil Justice Office
Pennsylvania Coalition Against Domestic Violence
6400 Flank Drive #1300, Harrisburg, PA 17112
Phone 717-671-4767 / 1-800-903-0111 ext. 2

The BWJP Defense Office
National Clearinghouse for the Defense of Battered Women
125 S. 9th Street #302, Philadelphia, PA 19107
Phone 215-351-0010 / 1-800-903-0111 ext. 3

The Black Church and Domestic Violence Institute
2740 Greenbriar Parkway #256, Atlanta, GA 30331
Phone 770-909-0715, Website www.bcdvi.org

Bureau of Justice Statistics Clearinghouse
810 Seventh Street NW, Washington, DC 20531
Phone 1-800-851-3420, Website www.ojp.usdoj.gov/bjs

CAAAV Organizing Asian Communities
2473 Valentine Avenue, Bronx, NY 10458
Website www.caaav.org

Child Welfare League of America
440 First Street NW, Third Floor, Washington, DC 20001
Phone 202-638-2952, Website www.cwla.org

Childhelp USA
15757 N. 78th Street, Scottsdale, AZ 85260
Phone 1-800-422-4453, Website www.childhelpusa.org

Children's Defense Fund
25 "E" Street NW, Washington, DC 20001
Phone 202-628-8787, Website www.childrensdefense.org

Coalition for Justice in the Maquiladoras
4207 Willow Brook, San Antonio, TX 78228
Phone 210-732-8957, Website www.coalitionforjustice.net

Equality Now
P.O. Box 20646, Columbus Circle Station, New York, NY 10023
Website www.equalitynow.org

Faith Trust Institute
2400 N. 45th Street #10, Seattle, WA 98103
Phone 206-634-1903, www.cpsdv.org

Family Violence Prevention Fund
383 Rhode Island Street #304, San Francisco, CA 94103
Phone 415-252-8900, TTY 1-800-595-4889, Website www.endabuse.
org

The Feminist Majority and the Feminist Majority Foundation
1600 Wilson Boulevard #801, Arlington, VA 22209, Phone 703-522-2214
433 S. Beverly Drive, Beverly Hills, CA 90212, Phone 310-556-2500
Website www.feminist.org

Graduate School of Public Affairs, University of Colorado
The Master's Program on Domestic Violence
Phone 1-800-990-8227 ext. 4182, Website www.cudenver.edu/gspa

Hate-Crime National Hotline, The Anti-Violence Project
Phone 208-246-2292

Human Rights Watch
350 Fifth Avenue, 34th Floor, New York, NY 10118
Website www.hrw.org

The Humane Society of the United States, First Strike Campaign
2100 "L" Street NW, Washington, DC 20037
Phone 1-888-213-0956, Website www.hsus.org/firststrike

INCITE! Women of Color Against Violence
Website www.incite-national.org

Indigenous Women's Network
13621 FM 78726, Austin, TX 78726
Phone 512-258-3880, Website www.indigenouswomen.org

Institute on Domestic Violence in the African American Community
University of Minnesota School of Social Work, College of Human Ecology
290 Peters Hall, 1404 Gortner Avenue, St. Paul, MN 55108
Phone 1-877-643-8222, Website www.dvinstitute.org

Jewish Women International
2000 "M" Street NW #720, Washington, DC 20036
Phone 1-800-343-2823, Website www.jewishwomen.org

JIST Life / KIDSRIGHTS
8902 Otis Avenue, Indianapolis, IN 46216
Phone 1-800-648-5478, Website www.jistlife.com

LAMBDA GLBT Community Services
216 S. Ochoa Street, El Paso, TX 79901
Phone 206-350-4283, Website www.lambda.org

Legal Momentum
395 Hudson Street, New York, NY 10014
Phone 212-925-6635, Website www.nowldef.org

Manavi
PO Box 3103, New Brunswick, NJ 08903
Phone 732-435-1414, Website www.manavi.org

Mending the Sacred Hoop - Technical Assistance Project
202 E. Superior Street, Duluth, MN 55802
Phone 1-888-305-1650, Website www.msh-ta.org

The Miles Foundation (violence and the military)
P.O. Box 423, Newton, CT 06470
Phone 203-270-7861, Website members.aol.com/milesfdn/myhomepage

Ms. Foundation for Women
120 Wall Street, 33rd Floor, New York, NY 10005
Phone 212-742-1653, Website www.ms.foundation.org

National Center for Elder Abuse
1201 - 15th Street NW #350, Washington, DC 20005
Phone 202-898-2586, Website www.elderabusecenter.org

National Center for Human Rights Education
P.O. Box 311020, Atlanta, GA 31131
Phone 404-344-9629

National Center for Victims of Crime
2000 M Street, NW, Suite 480, Washington, DC
Phone 202-467-8700, Website www.ncvc.org

National Center for Youth Law
405 - 14th Street, 15th Floor, Oakland, CA 94612
Phone 510-835-8098, Website www.youthlaw.org

National Center on Domestic and Sexual Violence
7800 Shoal Creek #120-N, Austin, TX 78757
Phone 512-407-9020, Website www.ncdsv.org

National Clearinghouse on Abuse in Later Life
Wisconsin Coalition Against Domestic Violence
307 S. Paterson Street #1, Madison, WI 53703
Phone 608-255-0539, Website www.ncall.us

National Clearinghouse on Child Abuse and Neglect Information
330 "C" Street SW, Washington, DC 20447
Phone 1-800-394-3366, Website nccanch.acf.hhs.gov

National Coalition for the Homeless
1012 Fourteenth Street NW #600, Washington, DC 20005
Phone 202-737-6444, Website www.nationalhomeless.org

National Coalition of Anti-Violence Programs
240 W. 35th Street #200, New York, NY 10001
Phone 212-714-1184, Website www.ncavp.org

National Domestic Violence Hotline
P.O. Box 161810, Austin, TX 78716
Phone 1-800-799-7233, TTY 1-800-787-3224, Website www.ndvh.org

National Gay and Lesbian Task Force
1325 Massachusetts Avenue NW #600, Washington, DC 20005
Phone 202-393-5177, Website www.ngltf.org

National Health Resource Center on Domestic Violence
Family Violence Prevention Fund
383 Rhode Island Street #304, San Francisco, CA 94103
Phone 1-888-792-2873, Website www.endabuse.org

National Immigration Forum
50 "F" Street NW #300, Washington, DC 20001
Phone 202-347-0040, Website www.immigrationforum.org

National Latino Alliance for the Elimination of Domestic
Violence (ALIANZA)
P.O. Box 672, Triborough Station, New York, NY 10035
Phone 646-672-1404, Website www.dvalianza.org

National Network for Immigrant and Refugee Rights
310 - 8th Street #303, Oakland, CA 94607
Phone 510-465-1984, Website www.nnirr.org

National Network to End Domestic Violence
660 Pennsylvania Avenue SE #303, Washington, DC 20003
Phone 202-543-5566, Website www.nnedv.org

National Organization for Victim Assistance
1730 Park Road NW, Washington, DC 20010
Phone 1-800-879-6682, Website www.try-nova.org

National Resource Center on Domestic Violence
Pennsylvania Coalition Against Domestic Violence
6400 Flank Drive #1300, Harrisburg, PA 17112
Phone 1-800-537-2238, TTY 1-800-553-2508, Website www.nrcdv.
org

National Runaway Switchboard
3080 N. Lincoln Avenue, Chicago, IL 60657
Phone 773-880-9860 / 1-800-621-4000, Website www.nrscrisisline.
org

National Sexual Violence Resource Center
123 N. Enola Drive, Enola, PA 17025
Phone 1-877-739-3895, TTY 717-909-0715, Website www.nsvrc.org

National Women's Political Caucus
1634 Eye St. NW #310, Washington, DC 20006
Phone 202-785-1100, Website www.nwpc.org

Planned Parenthood Federation of America
434 W. 33rd Street, New York, NY 10001
Phone 212-541-7800, Website www.plannedparenthood.org

Rape, Abuse & Incest National Network (RAINN)
635-B Pennsylvania Avenue SE, Washington, DC 20003
Phone 1-800-656-4673 ext. 3, Website www.rainn.org

Resource Center on Domestic Violence: Child Protection & Custody
National Council on Juvenile & Family Court Judges
P.O. Box 8970, Reno, NV 89507
Phone 1-800-527-3223, Website www.nationalcouncilfvd.org

Sacred Circle
National Resource Center to End Violence Against Native Women
722 Saint Joseph Street, Rapid City, SD 57701
Phone 1-877-733-7623

Soroptimist International of the Americas
1709 Spruce Street, Philadelphia, PA 19103
Phone 215-893-9000, Website www.soroptimist.org

STOPDV, Inc.
PO Box 1410, Poway, CA 92074
Phone 858-679-2913, Website www.stopdv.com

Violence Against Women Office, U.S. Department of Justice
10th and Constitution Avenue NW #5302, Washington, DC 20530
Phone 202-616-8994, Website www.ojp.usdoj.gov/vawo

Women's Independence Scholarship Program, The Sunshine Lady Foundation
4900 Randall Parkway #H, Wilmington, NC 28403
Phone 910-397-7742 / 1-866-255-7742, Website <u>www. sunshineladyfdn.org</u>

HOW AN ABUSER CAN DISCOVER YOUR INTERNET ACTIVITIES

email: if an abuser has access to your email account, he or she may be able to read your incoming and outgoing mail. if you believe your account is secure, make sure you choose a password he or she will not be able to guess.

If an abuser sends you threatening or harassing email messages, they may be printed and saved as evidence of this abuse. Additionally, the messages may constitute a federal offense. For more information on this issue, contact your local United States Attorney's Office.

history / cache file: if an abuser knows how to read your computer's history or cache file (automatically saved web pages and graphics), he or she may be able to see information you have viewed recently on the internet.

You can clear your history or empty your cache file in your browser's settings.*

- **Netscape:**

  Pulldown Edit menu, select Preferences. Click on Navigator on choose 'Clear History'. Click on Advanced then select Cache. Click on "Clear Disk Cache".

On older versions of Netcape: Pulldown Options menu. Select Network Options, Select Cache. Click on "Clear Disk Cache".

- **Internet Explorer:**

Pull down Tools menu, select Internet Options. On General page, under Temporary Internet Files, click on "Delete Files." If asked, check the box to delete all offline content. Still within the Temporary Internet Files section, click on Settings. (This next step may make it harder to navigate pages where you'd like your information to be remembered, but these remaining cookies do show website pages you have visited. Therefore, use your own judgment as to whether or not to take this next step). Click on "View Files." Manually highlight all the files (cookies) shown, then hit Delete. Close that window, then on General page under History section, click on "Clear History."

- **AOL:**

Pulldown Members menu, select Preferences. Click on WWW icon. Then select Advanced. Purge Cache.

Additionally, a victim needs to make sure that the "Use Inline Autocomplete" box is NOT checked. This function will complete a partial web address while typing a location in the address bar at the top of the browser.

If you are using Internet Explorer, this box can be found on the MS Internet Explorer Page by clicking on "Tools" at the top of the screen, then "Internet Options," and then the "Advanced" tab. About halfway down there is a "Use inline AutoComplete" box that can be checked and unchecked by clicking on it. Uncheck the box to disable the feature that automatically completes an internet address when you start typing in the internet address box.

* This information may not completely hide your tracks. Many browser types have features that display recently visited sites. The safest way to find information on the internet, would be at a local library, a friend's house, or at work.

Identifying Domestic Violence

What is Domestic Violence?

When spouses, intimate partners, or dates use physical violence, threats, emotional abuse, harassment, or stalking to control the behavior of their partners, they are committing domestic violence. Physical violence includes putting your hands on a person against their will. It also includes shoving, pushing, grabbing, pulling, or forcing some one to stay somewhere. Regardless of the relationship between two people, using physical violence against someone is a crime.

Very few people identify themselves as abusers or victims. They may remain silent about the issue because of the havoc that domestic violence has created in their workplace and family lives. Victims may be silent about the abuse because of embarrassment or shame, or for fear that their batterers will hurt them if they tell other people about the violence. Abusers may minimize their actions or blame the victims for provoking the violence. Both victims and abusers may characterize their experiences as family quarrels that "got out of control."

Think about the following questions to identify whether you or someone you know is a victim of domestic violence. Whether you are a professional or a friend, asking these questions (in private) about domestic violence can let victims or abusers know that the door is open for further discussion and help. If you or someone you know is being abused, develop a safety plan right away even if you do not intend to separate at this time.

Screening Questions

- Domestic violence is not confined to "certain groups." Do not try to predict who is a batterer and who is a victim of domestic violence. Ask the following questions to determine whether domestic violence is occurring.

- Everyone argues or fights with their partner or spouse now and then. When you argue or fight at home, what happens? Do you ever change your behavior because you are afraid of the consequences of a fight?

- Do you feel that your partner or spouse treats you well? Is there anything that goes on at home that makes you feel afraid?

- Has your partner or spouse ever hurt or threatened you or your children? Has your partner or spouse ever put their hands on you against your will? Has your partner or spouse ever forced you to do something you did not want to do? Does your partner or spouse criticize you or your children a lot?

- Has your partner or spouse ever tried to keep you from taking medication you needed or from seeking medical help? Does your partner refuse to let you sleep at night?

- Has your partner or spouse ever hurt your pets or destroyed your clothing, objects in your home, or something which you especially cared about? Does your partner or spouse throw or break objects in the home during arguments?

- Does your partner or spouse act jealously, for example, always calling you at work or home to check up on you? Is it hard for you to maintain relationships with your friends, relatives, neighbors, or co-workers because your partner or spouse disapproves of, argues with, or criticizes them? Does your partner or spouse accuse you unjustly of flirting with others or having affairs? Has your partner or spouse ever tried to keep you from leaving the house?

- Does your spouse or partner make it hard for you to find or keep a job or to go to school?

- Every family has their own way of handling finances. Does your partner or spouse withhold money from you when you need it? Do you know what your family's assets are? Do you know where important documents like bank books, check books, financial statements, birth certificates, and passports for you and members of your family are kept? If you wanted to see or use any of them, would your partner or spouse make it difficult for you to do so? Does your spouse or partner sometimes spend large sums of money and refuse to tell you why or what the money was spent on?

- Has your spouse or partner ever forced you to have sex or made you do things during sex that make you feel uncomfortable? Does your partner demand sex when you are sick, tired, or sleeping?

- Has your spouse or partner ever used or threatened to use a weapon against you? Are there guns in your home?

- Does your spouse or partner abuse drugs or alcohol? What happens?

Avoid Harmful Assumptions

- There are no typical characteristics or profiles of abusers or victims. Abusers may appear very charming or may seem like explosive or angry individuals. Victims may seem extremely frightened or passive or may be quite angry about what is happening. Rather than determining whether someone fits a "type," determine whether the warning signs of abuse exist.

- If some one declines to discuss domestic violence issues, consider whether the silence may be due to a fear of the batterer, or to cultural, race or gender issues which make it difficult to talk about such personal experiences. If you suspect that some one is a victim of domestic violence, say the following:

  o I am concerned about your safety.

  o You can talk to me about what is happening at home.

o   Domestic violence can harm your children.

o   Domestic violence is a crime.

o   I will help you find the legal and non-legal service referrals you need.

Basic Warning Signs

- Batterers use dominating, intimidating, terrifying, rule-making, stalking, harassing and injurious behaviors to control and manipulate the actions of their partners and sometimes their children.

- The most obvious signs of domestic violence will be evidence of severe, recurring, or life-threatening abuse, for example, repeated bruises, broken bones, physical attacks, or threats with weapons.

- Domestic violence is not just severe physical violence. It includes slaps, pushes, shoves, threats, emotional and financial abuse, false imprisonment, and any other behavior that batterers use to control and coerce victims. If one partner or spouse frequently makes the other ask permission to do things, domestic violence may be occurring.

- Emotional abuse, where one partner continuously degrades or belittles the other, or accuses the other of being stupid, unattractive, a bad parent, unfaithful, or any other similar fault, can indicate domestic violence.

- Many batterers use the legal system to punish their partners for taking steps to free themselves from domestic violence. Extremely litigious behavior following a separation may be a sign of domestic violence.

- Batterers use issues arising in custody and visitation cases to try to re-establish control over their victims. For example, a batterer may fail to show up for scheduled visitation on time in order to harass the victim or create a reason for further contact.

- Batterers frequently display extreme jealousy. The following controlling actions may signal that domestic violence is occurring:

o   Batterers often discourage their victims from seeking help. People who have difficulty making or keeping appointments may be trying to avoid letting their abusers know that they are seeking help.

o   Batterers frequently insist on accompanying victims to appointments, even if they have no involvement in the case. During office visits or phone calls, a batterer may try to speak for the victim, in order to control the information the victim shares with you.

o   Batterers harass, stalk, and keep tabs on their victims. If someone reports constant phone calls at work or home to keep track of their whereabouts, consider whether other warning signs of domestic violence are present.

o   Batterers try to isolate their victims from emotional support systems or sources of help. Be sensitive to persons who report that their partners do not allow them to see relatives, friends, or neighbors. Also, be alert for persons who tell you that their partners are excessively jealous of persons they see outside of the home and make statements such as "if I can't have you, nobody can."

o   Batterers also isolate their victims by sabotaging their ability to get and keep jobs. Clients who keep changing or losing jobs or "cannot" work because of their partners' disapproval or actions may be suffering from domestic violence.

SAFE HOUSES

AND

COUNSELING RESOURCES

FIGHTING ABUSE IN THE HOME (F.A.I.T.H.)

Mission statement: *To be a life-saving community resource that promotes a life free from abuse in any form.*

Fighting Abuse In The Home was founded by Rev. Bonita Chase Darby. This is a faith-based family violence resource ministry dedicated to training clergy and their congregations about signs and treatment of domestic violence.

The F.A.I.T.H. staff is available to schedule seminars and workshops to all faith communities.

For workshops and seminars contact:
Fighting Abuse In The Home
Campbell Chapel AME Church
100 E. 22nd Avenue
Denver, Co 80205
(303) 839-5058
fiaministries@msn.com

About SafeHouse Denver

Established in 1977, SafeHouse Denver is the only agency in the City of Denver that offers both shelter and non-residential support services specifically for victims of domestic violence. SafeHouse serves some 1,200 women and children each year through both our emergency shelter and our non-residential Counseling & Advocacy center. At both facilities, SafeHouse Denver offers individual counseling, support groups, safety planning, legal referral, and other support necessary to become safer, more confident and more self-sufficient. All our services are offered in both English and Spanish. SafeHouse Denver is committed to breaking the cycle of violence through our community education program, which offers training and information for schools, businesses and community groups. Additionally, we operate a 24-hour crisis and information line, 303-318-9989. For more information visit www.safehouse-denver.org.

Colorado Coalition Against Domestic Violence

The Mission of the National Coalition Against Domestic Violence is to organize for collective power by advancing transformative work, thinking and leadership of communities and individuals working to end the violence in our lives.

NCADV believes violence against women and children results from the use of force or threat to achieve and maintain control over others in intimate relationships, and from societal abuse of power and domination in the forms of sexism, racism, homophobia, classism, anti-Semitism, able-bodyism, ageism and other oppressions. NCADV recognizes that the abuses of power in society foster battering by perpetuating conditions, which condone violence against women and children. Therefore, it is the mission of NCADV to work for major societal changes necessary to eliminate both personal and societal violence against all women and children.

NCADV's work includes coalition building at the local, state, regional and national levels; support for the provision of community-based, non-violent alternatives - such as safe home and shelter programs - for battered women and their children; public education and technical assistance; policy development and innovative legislation; focus on the leadership of NCADV's caucuses and task forces developed to represent the concerns of organizationally under represented groups;

and efforts to eradicate social conditions which contribute to violence against women and children.

Principles of Unity

NCADV is comprised of people dealing with the concerns of battered women and their families. We represent both rural and urban areas. Our programs support and involve battered women of all racial, social, religious and economic groups, ages and lifestyles. We oppose the use of violence as a means of control over others and support equality in relationships and the concept of helping women assume power over their own lives. We strive toward becoming independent, community-based groups in which women make major policy and program decisions.

Summary of Organization's History

NCADV was formally organized in January 1978 when over 100 battered women's advocates from all parts of the nation attended the U.S. Commission on Civil Rights hearing on battered women in Washington, DC, hoping to address common problems these programs usually faced in isolation. NCADV, having celebrated 25 years in 2003, remains the only national organization of grassroots shelter and service programs for battered women.

In 1970, there was no such thing as a shelter for battered women. Today there are over 2,000 shelter and service programs, forming a national movement based on the belief that women and their children are entitled to a safe environment free from violence and the threat of violence.

Originally located in Washington, DC, NCADV opened a new office in Denver, Colorado in January 1992. The Colorado office now serves as the central office, while NCADV maintains a public policy office in Washington, DC.

Currently, a working Board of Directors comprised of caucus representatives and at-large members who are themselves active in domestic violence programs in their own communities govern NCADV. NCADV represents both rural and urban areas of the nation. Our programs involve and support battered women of all social, racial, ethnic, religious and economic groups, ages and lifestyles. Active caucuses include Battered/Formerly Battered Women, Women of Color, LBTGQQI, Jewish Women, Child and Youth Advocacy, Rural Women and Queer Persons of Color.

NCADV serves as a national information and referral center for the general public, media, battered women and their children, allied and member agencies and organizations. NCADV has a strong track record of providing programs with information and technical assistance, and has promoted the development of innovative programs, which address the special needs of all battered women, and the battered women's programs. NCADV has sponsored eleven National Conferences on domestic violence, which provide a unique forum within the battered women's movement for networking, dialogue, debate, leadership development and celebration.

NCADV also serves to impact public policy and legislation, which affects battered women and their children. NCADV organized testimony for the Attorney General's Task Force hearings on Family Violence; worked with federal legislators to develop priorities for Victims of Crime Act (VOCA) funds for battered women's programs; supported the development and passage of the Violence Against Women Act (1994); and was active in the passage of the Domestic Violence Offender Gun Ban (1996). www.ncadv.org

The Healing Club

Founded in 1995, the Healing Club is an online support community for domestic violence victims, survivors, and others who want to take part in the "healing" process or know someone who has been touched by domestic violence. The Healing Club is about "healing and rebuilding."

The Healing Club is a place where victims and survivors can network, get support, and obtain helpful resources which will provide them with tools to move forward to a healthier and happier life. The Healing Club is where people "heal and rebuild. Our goal for the Healing Club is to become the world's largest online domestic violence support community, and we are well on our way. Our goal is to play a key role in "ending the violence.

For further information, contact www.healingclub.com .

About the Author

Bonita Chase Darby once was trapped in the snares of domestic violence. For nine years, she endured the verbal and physical abuse of her spouse until the day he put a gun to her forehead, threatening to end her life and take their 7- year-old daughter. That day, on April 2, 1979 Bonita realized that this incident was part of a battle for her soul. During her ordeal, she regained the deep seated faith which had been planted by her mother and was able to move from the wilderness experience of domestic violence into the promised land of ministry.

Bonita Chase Darby is an ordained minister of the African Methodist Episcopal denomination. She is the Executive Director of Fighting Abuse In The Home, a resource ministry dedicated to providing much needed information to clergy and their congregations about family violence. Rev. Chase Darby travels to various faith communities facilitating seminars and family violence conferences. She considers herself a VICTOR, not a VICTIM and has dedicated her life to spreading words of hope to others who are in violent relationships.

Printed in the United States
62270LVS00004B/93